WELCOME HOME

Connecting with the Earth from within

by Sten Linnander

Copyright © 2016 by Sten Linnander

ISBN 978-3-9814889-9-9

Published by Sten Linnander, Enkheimer Str. 15, 60385 Frankfurt am Main, Germany. All rights reserved. No part of this publication may be reproduced, stored in a retrieval system, or transmitted in any form or by any means, electronic, mechanical, recording or otherwise, without the prior written permission of Sten Linnander.

Table of Contents

5	Introduction
8	About the author
18	A brief recap of the book *I Am With You*
23	So why a second book?
24	How I experience the communication
27	Personal note
27	Introduction by the Earth

31   Part I

Chapter 1. Co-Creation
- 34   What is co-creation and how does it work?
- 40   Individual and collective
- 42   Befriending the Unknown

Chapter 2. Co-thinking
- 45   A Family of One
- 46   From "We" to a new "I"
- 47   Difficulties
- 49   Our true "I"
- 50   So what is this new "I" like?

Chapter 3. Co-Visioning
59   Vision
63   Co-visioning

Chapter 4. Equity
67   Same, same, but different
73   Tat Tvam Asi
74   Dewdrops

81   PART II

Chapter 5. Q & A
83   How are you doing, Earth?
87   How can we connect with you?
97   What can we do to support you?
104 Tsunamis, earthquakes and other natural disasters
115 Love and sexuality
119 Birth and the Earth
122 Final Words

Introduction

The Earth is alive. She not only acts like a living system as the Gaia Theory[1] states, but she is also alive and conscious, like you and me. She has emotions and can feel what we feel. If we pay attention, we can feel her all the time, too. For we live inside of her, since the atmosphere and her energy fields that reach far into space are part of her. She wants to communicate with us, to talk with us as partners, not just as "children of the Earth." She says she wants us to cooperate consciously and that that will change everything, both for us and for her. For us an entirely new future would open up, and it would be like falling in love with everything in our surroundings.

The thoughts above are condensed from a book I wrote in 2011 entitled *I Am With You: The Earth Wants to Talk with Us*[2], describing experiences I had "speaking" with the Earth. In 2015 I was again "asked" by the Earth to write a second book, this

---

1 The Gaia Theory, developed by Dr. James Lovelock and Dr. Lynn Margulis, states that the Earth and its natural cycles can be thought of like a living organism. When one natural cycle starts to go out of kilter, other cycles work to bring it back, continually optimizing the conditions for life on Earth.
2 See www.IAmWithYou.com

time deepening the statements in the first book and answering questions I or others have.

This time around the Earth speaks of how we co-create our reality, how we can learn to think together with the Earth and how we can co-envision a beautiful future. What emerges is the promise of fulfilling a deeply held longing - a longing we are usually not even aware of. It is the longing of coming home here on Earth; of connecting intimately with the Earth and everything in our surroundings; of touching the Earth, the sky, the plants, animals and people both from within and without. I am not talking about a short-lived meditation experience, a mystical union or an unworldly blissful state, but rather a sober, relaxed yet quietly exciting state of intimate connectedness, which includes sharing thoughts, dreams and ideas as well as feelings and emotions. The practical possibilities that open up through conscious communication with the Earth are in essence limitless, and they touch all areas of our lives.

This shift in how we connect with the Earth and our surroundings goes hand in hand with a new way of seeing ourselves. Throughout the ages our sense of self has increasingly been encased in our physical form. By discovering the functional principles of the living world – how trees communicate with each other, how ant colonies self-organize, or swarms of birds or bees operate as single organisms – we are beginning to awaken to our own embeddedness in a greater living whole. As we allow this embeddedness to be experienced and felt consciously, and enter into intimate communication with all of nature and the Earth itself, our sense of self expands.

This expansion of our feeling of who we are is, in a sense, also a homecoming. We begin to touch the world around us from within, realizing there is no limit to the intimacy with which we can relate to each other, to nature, to the Earth. These are experiences of becoming whole again, for we thereby access deeper and more encompassing parts of ourselves and find our place in the network of the living world. At the same time, our individuality is strengthened, for it also means that the individual melody we play in the orchestra of life becomes more pure as we connect with others. The security and confidence we gain through connectedness lessens our fear and promotes the development of uniqueness and individuality.

The intent of this book is to nudge us toward making such experiences on our own, beginning by opening up to the possibility that we are much more deeply connected with the Earth than we usually think. In a sense this book is an instruction manual for connecting with the Earth, thinking with the Earth, and literally creating a future together with the Earth.

The more we allow for this possibility and the more we realize that we are truly not alone – that we are seen, felt and held by the Earth, all the time, and embedded in an unseen web of communication and exchange in which we can participate consciously – the more we can relax. After wandering disconnected on the Earth for so long, we are finally, in the deepest sense of the word, beginning to come home.

About the author

Since what I am writing about is somewhat unusual and based on experiences I have had, I feel the reader needs to know a bit about who I am. I have described my life and my background in some detail in my previous book, so I shall try to repeat myself as little as possible. I will also include some stories from my life that led me to be open to world views that are different from those I was taught to believe in as I was growing up.

I was born in Sweden on July 4, 1950 to a father who was an aspiring judge and a mother who was a secretary and language teacher. My parents were very adventurous and had spent two years in Ethiopia at the end of the 1940s, where my brother and sister were born. Having later served as a judge and legal advisor working for the United Nations in various countries, my father ultimately became a senior judge in Stockholm and an international arbitration judge. My mother taught languages, worked for the Swedish Red Cross and Save the Children, and then spent the last twenty years of her life establishing and running an international non-profit organization for the abolition of harmful traditional practices, focusing on female circumcision in Africa and elsewhere.

At the age of six, my world changed abruptly. We packed up and left for Kabul, Afghanistan, where my father worked for the government, helping them set up a functioning legal system. We stayed there two and a half years. Afghanistan was already a forbidding place by then, and my memories are of a fiercely proud people (actually men, for during my time there I never saw the face of a single Afghan woman) and high walls. I started my schooling there in an international school for children from all over the world.

After a year back in Sweden, we set off again, this time to Kathmandu, Nepal, for three and a half years. I first went to a Jesuit school for Nepalese children for a year and then to the American Lincoln School of Kathmandu. For me, Nepal was in many ways like a fairyland. The genuine friendliness and openness of the Nepalese people and the fresh natural beauty of the country I experienced in the early Sixties contrasted strongly with the unsmiling, stressful and complicated life in the West, where I had come from. Nepal is still my favorite country on Earth and I go back there to replenish my spirit about once every ten years.

All this meant that I got a global outlook on life at an early age, and it has stayed with me. I also realized that whatever world view I had, it was only one of a myriad of world views, and I noticed that most people simply took on what their parents and their culture taught them to believe. Since logic dictated that mine was therefore not necessarily the "best" or "truest" world view, I increasingly questioned what I learned and was always open to new perspectives.

Back in Sweden, I continued my schooling and at the tender age of thirteen, together with young women aspiring to become secretaries, I took evening classes to learn to type fast with all ten fingers. This skill has come in handy throughout my life. One example…. When I was nineteen, my father, together with two other legal experts, was asked secretly by King Idris of Libya to write a Western-style constitution for his country, which he wanted to promulgate in September 1969. My father asked me to type the Constitution in its many versions, amending it often depending on the wishes of the King. So I made my first real money on a Remington travel typewriter, making five copies with carbon paper, and at the same time learning a lot about constitutions. Sadly, these efforts came to naught when Muammar Gaddafi got wind of the King's plans and deposed him. Even historians do not seem to know of this background to Gaddafi's coup.

Later in life, since I always followed my interests as opposed to any particular career, I realized I needed a source of income that did not tie me to any specific place. This led to my becoming a translator, which is how I have made a living for the last several decades.

I finished high school, did my military service and then got a degree in physics and geophysics from Stockholm University. I was hoping my studies of physics, of matter and energy, would give me some insights about the nature of reality, the reality that surrounded me and that I was even made of. However, after a few years of study, I realized that physics, although creating a vast amount of theories and laws about creation, many of which could be "verified" to a very high degree of accuracy, only takes into account a tiny spectrum of the aspects that we associate with reality, and it does this in a highly abstract way. By eliminating any "human" qualities, such as consciousness, emotions and thinking, physics takes "life" out of its description and analysis of reality. This did not satisfy me, so I changed course in midstream to study geophysics. It was like going from theory to reality, suddenly trying to understand lightning storms, the dramatic history of the Earth, the importance of wetlands and river deltas. I reveled in plumbing the depths of the oceans and watching in my inner eye as continental plates crashed into each other, resulting in mountain ranges the size of the Himalayas or the Alps. Although the language was still scientific, somehow the Earth came alive to me. Yet I knew that I would not become a professional geophysicist, for there was something deeper calling me, something that had more to do with immersing myself in reality and entering into a living relationship with everything around me.

Beginning as a teenager, I took an interest in existential questions, such as spirituality, Eastern religions, parapsychology, esoteric teachings, and many other fields. Out of a feeling that "this can't be all there is," I devoured much literature about such issues, fascinated by Ram Dass and his spiritual odyssey through Nepal and India, studying the Vedic book *Bhagavata Purana*, dealing with Bhakti Yoga (or "loving devotion"); but also taking an interest in the existential therapy methods of the time with their corresponding philosophies, among them Primal Therapy by Arthur Janov and Gestalt Therapy by Fritz Perls.

Yet I was not really part of the counter-culture, and I remember quite vividly during my time in the military the reception that I and my best friend got when we went to see the musical *Hair*. To get to the performance on time, we did not have the opportunity to change clothes, so we went to the theater in uniform, not knowing that the actors wandered around the theater during the performance, engaging the audience in conversation and fun. Of course, we got more than our share of attention!

All the books by Carlos Castaneda, describing various teachings about "separate realities," supposedly taught by a Toltec shaman called Don Juan, fascinated me no end; and whether or not these books are fact or fiction, they awakened in me a curiosity that influenced me later in life. The books by Jane Roberts, a trance medium who channeled an energy personality called Seth, also greatly colored my world view. In short, Seth says that we create our own reality and that our beliefs generate emotions which trigger our memories and organize our associations. Eventually those beliefs manifest in our physical lives and health.

Not sure of what I wanted to do with my life and being quite depressed, I tried straightening myself out with Gestalt Therapy sessions and various other techniques. But I soon realized I needed much stronger methods if I was ever to crawl out of my self-imposed shell. So I joined a radical and controversial commune in Austria called the AAO, with common property, free sexuality, spontaneous self-expression performances for four to five hours daily, various forms of art and a kind of intense energetic therapy they had developed on their own, based on the ideas of Wilhelm Reich. Although I strongly disagreed with much of what went on there, for me it was a time of inner cleansing. After three years I left, feeling liberated and ready to begin my life anew. Some eight years after I left, the group imploded; the founder and leader went to jail for sex with minors; and the group, which by then had some thousand members scattered in smaller groups all over Europe, was dissolved.

During the last year of my stay in the commune I was sent to Denmark to act as a kind of group leader in one of the smaller groups. I was also expected to introduce the newest forms of spontaneous self-expression, which entailed using light hypnosis as a way of liberating deeper emotional blocks. The members of the Danish group suggested trying out hypnosis as a way of accessing memories from "past lives," although this was definitely not part of the belief system of the Austrian commune. But I agreed, and we tried it out with some of the members of the group. The result was a number of astonishing stories from centuries bygone, or sometimes from "lives" that ended just a few years before their current lives began. Not knowing what to believe, I later researched several of these stories in depth, finding corresponding historical details that were so deeply buried in specialist literature that the young members of the commune could not have known about them.

In the group there was a nineteen-year-old woman, who had grown up in a small town in Greenland until she was fifteen and never finished high school. It was very easy to put her into a deep trance, during which she did not know that she was under hypnosis. Instead, she identified fully with the person in her "past life," the most prominent one being a baron in Portugal who in 1525 went by ship to Macau in China to trade in silk. Later I traveled to Portugal to research this case and found that many obscure details in her story were historically correct.

One evening she had fallen asleep on a sofa in the living room, when suddenly she began to speak with her eyes closed. At first I did not understand what she was saying, but then I realized she was speaking in French. I answered in French and it turned out that she thought she was a four-year-old boy in Portugal – the same person who grew up to become the baron who went to China. We talked – in French – for about half an hour and she told me stories from her life, including that she had an instructor who taught her French. Later, when she woke up, she had forgotten our conversation and, to my amazement, she told me she didn't know a word of French. This was confirmed by others in the group who knew her well.

This was the beginning of a series of about 100 hypnotic regressions that I guided various people through, most of them after I left the commune. I slowly began to believe that we at least in some sense have lived before. But having read a fair amount of the literature about supposed reincarnation, and considering the many stories of those who claimed to have been Cleopatra or some other important person in history, I was also open to other explanations: for example, that the human mind has the ability to access knowledge of events from other people's lives and "remember" them as if they were their own.

In any case, having left the Austrian commune in 1980, I spent the better part of three years applying for patents and marketing new inventions by a German inventor in the United States. Among other things, they constituted highly effective, proven methods for cleaning oily waste water and ridding the air in coal mines of the micron-sized particles that cause black lung disease. Here, I gained my first insights into the less than honorable business methods used by many companies and individuals.

During this time I also got involved with a German community called the Bauhütte (which later split into two projects: ZEGG in Germany and Tamera in Portugal), founded by the sociologist and author Dr. Dieter Duhm, whom I had met and befriended in the Austrian commune. The idea behind this experimental project was to bring together the most innovative and future-oriented ideas, methods, world views, etc. and apply them in the creation of a living model community. All areas of life were to be represented, including "outer" topics such as ecology, energy production, architecture and healing, and "inner" issues such as competition, love, sex, jealousy, and transparency within the group. Major focuses were also placed on art, music and spiritual endeavors, and we experimented with communication with plants, dowsing and spiritual technologies of various kinds. We invited people from all over the world to talk about their research and their knowledge and organized practical workshops to implement what we learned, to continue the research and develop further ideas of our own. As an example, the focus of one such workshop was to connect so deeply with stinging nettles, of which there were plenty on the property, that one could touch them and even roll around in them without getting stung. Many of the things we did entailed going beyond the boundaries of our belief systems, opening ourselves up to new possibilities.

I was a part of this project until 1994. My own role was one of introducing new world view perspectives and spiritual ideas, on one hand by inviting leading-edge thinkers from the fields of science, spirituality, biology, interspecies communication, etc. to share their research with us. Within the framework of what we called the "Free University," I invited people such as Rupert Sheldrake, the originator of the theory of morphic resonance; Peter Caddy, the founder of the spiritual Findhorn Community; the geomancy expert Nigel Pennick; Cleve Backster, with his experiments purporting to show that plants react to human intentions; and many more. On the other hand, we pursued various projects of our own at the intersection between spirit and matter. I also introduced trance methods that ultimately had the aim of softening our rigid beliefs about how the world works and who we are.

A special interest of mine concerned the theory of "Energy Synthesis" by the late industrial designer and artist Alfred Wakeman. Energy Synthesis is a fluid dynamic theory of the Universe. It assumes that there is an underlying medium of all existence, seeing an atom as a self-preserving "storm" of recirculation of this subatomic fluid medium. Energy Synthesis presents a fascinating world view of a living universe, including regarding thoughts and emotions as consisting of motions of the same underlying medium as that underlying our material world. I worked with Alfred Wakeman for thirty years, until his death, running experiments based on his theory, and I am now about to restart this work.

In 1989, while still with this project, I and two friends started a non-profit organization called "Aktion Perestroika." For three years we organized various technical and humanitarian aid projects for the people of the former Soviet Union, as they were experiencing great hardships associated with the massive changes the country was going through. We organized truckloads of aid and initiated energy-saving projects for the city of Moscow, set up a model birth clinic, and arranged for city councilmen in Moscow to visit German cities to learn how cities are run in the West. One project close to my heart came about when the Association of Cities of Northwest Russia asked us to coordinate a project to get cities around the Arctic to demand that the Arctic be declared a nuclear-free zone. It was when working on this project, which I called "Haven Arctica," that I began to sense that the Earth is alive and conscious, and that the Arctic is a very sensitive and important place on Earth. Yet it took another sixteen years before I "heard" the Earth speaking to me.

In 1994 I and my beloved wife Karin, whom I had met in 1983 and married in 1988, left the German project for Phoenix, Arizona. In 1992 I began studying the spiritual-shamanic teachings of the "Sweet Medicine Sundance Path," an eclectic synthesis of the knowledge of medicine men and women of the Americas and Australia that also incorporates modern scientific and psychological insights. This path consists of a step-by-step process of "gateways," with both theoretical teachings and practical ceremonies. It provided me with a fascinating, highly structured worldview, together with powerful ceremonies, most of them out in nature, based on these teachings. This path, which I pursued for over seventeen years, gave me many tools for attaining various states of consciousness and becoming a more conscious master of my own life. It also greatly expanded my world view to incorporate spiritual beings of various kinds and gave me an awareness of the limitless powers of the mind that slumber in all of us. I had numerous experiences that indicated that what we do in our minds affects reality directly.

It was in September 1996, during one of the ceremonies on this path, that I unexpectedly experienced seeing in my inner eye a beautiful image of our blue planet and hearing it speak to me. In essence, I was asked to go up on a mountain in the Phoenix area and, without any preparations, simply talk with the Earth. I highly doubted if this would yield anything, but to my surprise, having soon thereafter climbed a small mountain in Phoenix, the "conversation" started up again with the same clear quality as during the ceremony. This led to a series of exchanges, 2-3 times a week for three months, during which I also promised to publish what I received. For various reasons it then took me another fifteen years before I finally decided to fulfill that promise. I rented a cottage out in nature and spent a few months in 2011 re-establishing contact with the Earth and writing the book *I Am With You: The Earth Wants to Talk with Us.*[3] By now, it has been published and is available in English, German, Spanish and French.

A brief recap of the book *I Am With You.*

The Earth introduces herself as an alive and conscious being. She lets us know she is with us all the time, she can feel what we are going through, and she also has emotions of her own that we feel. These emotions are real; they exist as real "things." She tells us we are truly living within her body, because she consists not only of solid matter, but her atmosphere and energy fields, which extend far out into space, are a part of her. This means that we are not living "on Earth"; we are actually living "in the Earth." This became more real to me as I realized that if we see the atmosphere as part of the Earth's "body," then we are constantly breathing in and out a part of the Earth herself. In her own words: "In a very real way, you are inside of me. You are breathing my air. As a species you have decided to come into me, and I have welcomed you."

---

3 See www.IAmWithYou.com

The Earth tells us we can feel she is with us all the time; we can feel her energies in our bodies, and she is asking us to start communicating with her consciously from within. She is, so to speak, calling us on the phone, waiting for us to pick up the receiver.

She says that in a sense we are her children, and she has nurtured us for eons. But now we are growing up, going through a kind of collective adolescence, and she addresses us as an equal partner. And she wants us to establish a deep relationship with her and with the living world around us.

> *Earth:*
>
> *The more You are aligned with me,*
> *the more we act as one,*
> *in harmony with each other.*
>
> *So I am not asking You*
> *to change Your thoughts or actions.*
>
> *I am asking You to enter into*
> *a living relationship with me.*

The image she presents is that we humans have chosen to come to Earth and that she attracted us, just as we attracted her. Through us, she can see herself and her beauty, and she needs humans to let her do that. We humans were on a quest to discover new parts of ourselves and "play in new gardens." She says that in our everyday lives we do not allow our energies to flow freely through our minds and bodies; but when we start to feel her presence, we allow her into us and connect with her flows. We then start acting as one organism.

So the Earth tells us that we, as non-physical beings, have come from elsewhere in the Universe and that we had one common goal: Allowing, or combining, freedom and intimacy. At first this sounds like an unusual goal for a planet to share with the human species, but anybody who has been in a relationship knows that these are quite important qualities that are not easy to combine. She goes on to explain what this could mean both for the Earth and for us.

According to the Earth, her interactions with the Sun are like that of a lover, and she likens the various hours of the day with good lovemaking (see Chapter 5). She also says: My connection with the Sun, my lovemaking with the Sun, began a process of conscious awakening in me. The material expression of this awakening was the first forms of life on Earth."[4]

The Earth says that she is a highly sexual being and that she reacts to our sexual energies. Here, sexuality is not seen as being limited to physical sex, but includes enthusiasm, creativity, arousal and exuberance. So every time we become aroused, enthused or creative, she comes up to meet our energies. She

---

[4] Some five years after I wrote my book, studies by NASA scientists were published, claiming that life on Earth may have originated as a result of "superflares" from the Sun about 4 billion years ago which seeded life-supporting molecules that are crucial for creating DNA. See https://www.sciencenews.org/article/young-sun's-super-solar-flares-helped-set-early-earth-life

says we will notice this when we make love in outer space, for her energies will not be there in the same way.

Furthermore, both she and nature are waiting for us to enter into an entirely new sexual state of being. When we connect with the Earth in a sexual way, she becomes something like an incubator for our desires or visions, a process similar to when a man and a woman come together to conceive a child.

She speaks of trust and says that trust is not passively letting happen what happens, but rather actively taking responsibility for what happens by "exuding, insisting on, being received." We also hear of beauty and power, and that beauty is a seed of true strength that will harness all other forces and turn them into her service.

If we let these thoughts awaken inside our bodies, something starts to happen. We start to open up, and it is this opening up that is needed to enter into a new form of communication with the Earth.

She goes on to say that everything that has transpired on Earth is recorded in everything on Earth. She wants to show us our true history on Earth, for we need to see the past in order to be able to move forward. For this reason she wants us to develop a device whereby she can speak to us in our own language, and also show us images, even videos; and she provides the basic principles involved in building such a device.

She speaks of the weather as the swirling of her emotions, and the Moon as having healing powers, emphasizing the importance of both women and men connecting with the Moon. She stretches our imagination when she speaks of time not being linear, nor circular or simultaneous, saying instead that time is an event. According to her, our disconnected view of time, which she describes as being due to a resistance against events, has infiltrated our way of creating the world around us in such a way that it reinforces the separation already there. But she also says we can and will learn to communicate through time and even "jump" through time, not because we need to do so for our survival, but because we are beings who are discovering our own abilities and excitement and because humans are ultimately not bound by time and space.

So what would it be like if we had a conscious, intimate connection with the Earth? In her own words....

Earth:

*I am so much a part of the reality
that surrounds You that a shift in how You see me
can be like falling in love, head over heels,
with everything in Your surroundings.*

*True cooperation between humans and me,
the Earth, will leave no area untouched.*

*I want to give You what You need and want,
and so much more.*

> *Yet You have acted like thieves,*
> *breaking into a palace, raiding the kitchen,*
> *stealing the silverware, vandalizing the*
> *living quarters and burning the place down,*
> *for You could not believe*
> *that the palace was there for You*
> *to come and live in, in luxury.*

Finally, she makes it clear that it is up to us and she will not force herself upon us. Instead, she is holding out a hand of cooperation, and asks us to allow for the possibility that we are deeply connected from within. She wants us to know that a conscious connection, both collectively and individually, is not only possible but also deeply desired on her part. Her request of the reader is that he/she go out into nature – or even a park – find a quiet place, undisturbed, and commune with her in whatever way comes naturally.

So why a second book?

Having published *I Am With You*, I felt that my part had been done and I did not plan to write another book. This changed in April of 2015 when I was staying alone at a ranch in the desert of Arizona. Early one beautiful, pristine morning, as I was sitting outside drinking a cup of coffee, I had the urge to connect with the Earth. When I felt that contact had been made, I asked if she had anything to tell me. The answer came quickly: "Yes, I would like you to write another book." This took me totally by surprise.

When I asked what the second book should be about, she suggested it be a deepening of the first book, and also that it be based on questions that either I or others have. So in the months that followed I sent out letters to some twenty people whom I knew and who had read my book and could relate to it, asking if they would send me any questions they might have of the Earth. I got plenty of answers and have included several of them in Chapter 5 of this book.

As was the case for the first book, I again felt the need to spend time alone out in nature to connect with the Earth and write this book. I had access to an isolated summer house at a lake close to Stockholm, Sweden, and I spent two months there the summer of 2015 communing with the Earth and collecting material. This was a beautiful and powerful time for me, and I felt the Earth and nature spoke to me in many different ways.

How I experience the communication

During my first communications with the Earth back in 1996, I experienced the Earth as a separate being, speaking to me "in my head." I tried my utmost to keep my own thoughts out of the process, since I felt this would taint anything the Earth wished to communicate. At the same time, I was aware that I could probably only receive something that in some way fit my own thinking, my own view of reality and my own values.

Later, in 2011, as I was writing the book *I Am With You*, compiling what I received in 1996 and asking further questions of the Earth, I was specifically asked to change the way I received what the Earth said. I was told to simply connect as deeply as I could with the Earth, pose the questions I had and see what thoughts emerged. I was told that this way of communicating conformed more to what actually was happening.

This time, in 2015, as described in Chapter 2, I was first asked to connect with the Earth to become a thinking "we," and then to let this "we" morph into an "I." The idea was thus not to experience myself as separate from the Earth, nor as a part of the Earth, but as a being consisting of the sum of myself and the Earth. This was quite a challenge. Another challenge, which remained a difficulty throughout the writing of this book, concerned the form that the thoughts that arose then took. Often, the thoughts that came to me were formulated from the perspective of the Earth, saying things like "I, the Earth…" But quite a few times the thoughts were formulated from the human perspective, such as "When we grow older …" The form could sometimes even vary within two consecutive sentences. Rather than afterwards changing these thoughts so as to be formulated consistently in one way or the other, I let them stand as they came to me. This may give rise to some confusion about who is really speaking or thinking; but please keep in mind that, as I experienced it, it was a conglomerate of the Earth and myself that was writing this book, sometimes choosing to formulate thoughts from the perspective of the Earth, and sometimes making statements about us human beings as "we."

This book deals very much with how we can connect with the Earth, how we can create, think, envision and commune with the Earth. I expected the writing to be fairly easy and straightforward, but this was not so. Almost every session required a change in my belief system that altered my way of thinking about myself and my way of relating to my surroundings, to others and to the Earth. It was also an emotional roller coaster, often going from a feeling of not understanding and not being able to get clear answers to questions that I and others had, to doubt – not doubt that the Earth is alive, but doubt about the clarity of my connection to her. And then, again and again, I experienced the feeling of deep gratitude and excitement when new possibilities opened up.

As I said, asking the Earth questions was sometimes frustrating for me, for I seldom got direct answers. At times it felt like interviewing a politician who never gives straight answers. But more and more I realized that the answers were designed to shift or expand the framework of the question, leading me or the reader to think in a new way. And thinking in a new way often let me see that the way I had asked the question was only relevant from a disconnected point of view. I once asked the Earth about what to do about this lack of straight answers. She answered: "Let the book be exactly that. The book should draw in, spin around, and go back out. This is the principle of evolution. Evolution is not 'straightforward' and spinning is central to the Universe."

Once in a while throughout this book, I will share with the reader the process whereby it was written, especially since the way it came about illustrates many of the thoughts that the Earth is trying to get across. This includes some of the difficulties I encountered as I tried to implement what I learned.

Early on, I asked the Earth if she had any suggestions regarding the structure of the book, and she said that, in addition to including a number of questions and answers, I should have one chapter about co-creation, one about co-thinking, one about co-visioning and one about what she called "equity." With "equity" she means something like "of equal value." Not exactly equality or of equal importance, but rather that any choice of perspective is equally valid, combined with the freedom to be different without value judgment. Equity also means that that there is a natural way for anything in the Universe, whether small or large, to communicate with any other thing as an equal.

Personal note

Although I have always felt that the Earth was a female being and I did not doubt that the Earth is conscious, I always hesitated calling her "she," and in *I Am With You* I always only referred to "the Earth" or "it." Over the years, as my connection with the Earth has become more intimate, this hesitation has melted away, and thinking of the Earth as a "she" feels right.

Introduction by the Earth

I am back again to deepen my connection not only with Sten, but with all the readers. This is an experimental project, as are all true projects. When we talk – when I talk to you, the reader – we are already connected, not just energetically, but also in conscious communication. Sten here plays the role that his original ceremony played for him, during which he heard me speak. You now hear me speak through him; but in reality I am speaking directly to you. I hope this will become more obvious to you as we continue.

As I see it, you are "buzzing" all the time. This buzzing is the communication that is going on between you and your world. Mostly, your buzzing is between you and other people. Only sometimes do you buzz what I call "vertically," meaning to your source, i.e. to the consciousness source from where you come, from the deeper parts of you that you are connected to – to me, the Earth, and to the non-human world, of which you are a part. You are not only human; you also consist of what you would call non-human elements. But not dead elements, for there is no such thing as a dead element.

My aim with this book is to draw humans ever closer to me by describing what we are doing all the time together, in order that we might start to do these things together **consciously**. You will then understand the level of connectedness we not only already have, but that we are seeking to harmonize and make conscious, based on what I see as a form of lovemaking, in which we recognize that we have chosen to come together to act as one. This choice has been made at several levels, from the highest universal level, to the level of humans as a collective and me the Earth, down to the level of each individual human being and me. It is not only related to you and me, the Earth; it is also a quest for humans to recognize each other in this sense; and ultimately to recognize who you are, yourselves, as the whole.

> *Earth:*
>
> *My intent is for humans and me*
> *to enter into a partnership.*
>
> *This is a partnership that you cannot*
> *"will" to make happen.*
>
> *You cannot will yourself to love or fall in love.*
>
> *But you can, slowly, gently and consistently,*
> *unclench the fist around your heart.*
>
> *To use an image that is yours…*
>
> *When waking up in the morning,*
> *looking your lover in his or her eyes,*
> *relaxing into that gaze into each other,*
> *something happens within you –*
> *an opening is created, a flow is allowed,*
> *and all is good.*
>
> *That is how close I am to you.*

This second book builds on statements in the first book. It goes further and deeper and is more of a stretch of both the imagination and what is asked of the reader. I want you to enter into a conversation with me, either in the form of thoughts or out loud, for speaking out loud is a good way of making what is not yet conscious, conscious. Thoughts expressed, either in the vaults of your mind or out loud, move evolution forward, as does silence with awareness.

I am with you now. Once your cells and your mind open up to my presence, a love relationship begins; and this relationship is like a great adventure that opens up new horizons for both of us. I thank you, the reader, for being open to these thoughts and for letting me into your life.

PART I

Chapter 1. Co-Creation

Making it up

Back in 1996, when I was beginning to communicate with the Earth on the top of a small mountain in Phoenix, Arizona, I was sitting there one day, relaxing after having climbed the mountain, about to try to communicate with the Earth. Without any specific intent, I found myself fantasizing about a scene in a movie in which a young man walking on the street meets an old, wrinkled Native American medicine man who challenges him to race to the top of a nearby mountain (the one I was sitting on) – the winner to get $5. The young guy is sure he'll win and takes him up on it. So they set off, taking different paths; and when the young man arrives at the summit, out of breath, he sees the old man sitting there, quietly waiting for him. To distract from his sense of failure,

> the young man says simply, "We made it up." The medicine man smiles and replies, "Yes, we made it up. But then again, we make everything up!" So begins a series of teachings by the medicine man. To this day I have no idea where that story came from.

As I began to write this book and asked my first question, I got a sense of what this book was all about. I started out by asking, "Earth, are you there?" When I got the answer, "I am always with you," I followed up with, "OK, will you help me write this book?" The answer I got was, "No, *we* are writing this book." And yet it was not until much later that I realized that the "we" the Earth was talking about was more than the sum of the two of us and required that I let go of my sense of self, embracing and in a sense becoming a "we," that in turn became an "I" that was novel to me.

What is co-creation and how does it work?

Earth: Conscious co-creation first entails letting go of your hardened belief systems about reality. When I say hardened, I do not mean it in any derogatory sense. Hardened simply means having become "hard" through constant repetition. You are used to seeing three-dimensional reality, and even your emotional reality to a lesser degree, as a given. When you look around, you see and can touch your most immediate environment; and you can become aware of the greater reality encompassing the whole Earth, the planets, stars and ultimately the whole Universe. This is the backdrop against which you see your lives being lived out. This is one way of seeing it, and again, there is nothing wrong in that. Yet when you see reality in this way, you are not aware of creating it. It seems to you as if reality exists independent of you, your thinking, your emotions, etc. You are only aware of being able to change your reality through physical interaction. The furthest you go is developing devices whereby your thoughts can give rise to physical actions.[5]

Everything makes models of itself.[6] So in a sense your technologies are a reverse engineering of yourselves. You also do this when you make movies consisting of individual images that you string together to awaken the illusion that they are continuous. It is, however, the stringing together of the images and projecting them in a certain sequence onto a screen that makes them seem real to you. There is no difference in principle between such a movie and the appearance of your three-dimensional physical reality.

Your entire three-dimensional world, including the entire physical Universe, which you experience as being fairly fixed, is only fixed under certain circumstances. Under other inner circumstances, however, and with a different kind of perception, it is as fluid and changeable as chaos itself. In essence, reality is even more fluid than what you experience in dreams, for in a dream you still retain a semblance of continuity that you are not aware of creating. You choose this because you are infatuated

---

5 Examples of this are devices controlled with the help of headsets that read brain waves.
6 This is a saying by Alfred Wakeman, the developer of the Theory of Energy Synthesis.

with the story itself. To tell a story you need continuity; and you love stories, just like you love movies.

Sten: So how can one change one's perception to make this material world become more fluid than it seems, and is it even desirable? And how do we create reality all the time?

Earth: To answer the second question first, if it is desirable or not is determined by the perceiver, and you will only wish to perceive things differently if you sense the great opportunity that lies in doing so. Your habitual way of perceiving is indeed very precise. Your scientists will confirm this, since your ears and eyes can normally only perceive sounds and electromagnetic waves within a narrow window of frequencies. The same is true of your other senses that are the buildings blocks for you to perceive outer reality. There are, however, many other inner processes that are necessary for you to see reality the way you perceive it. In a sense, you choose to "assemble" your reality so that it in some ways makes sense to you. There are many other realities or dimensions surrounding you all the time, some of them "waiting" for you to perceive them. What you seldom realize is that there exists a level of thought from where you can select or enter into other modes of reality than what you are used to. You also go seamlessly in and out of different modes of perception which are also modes of creation of reality.

In spite of this, you are constantly reinforcing the way you see reality as separate from yourselves. This is a part of what you could call "having stepped out of paradise," for you no longer see yourself as being intimately connected to everything else.

You are always co-creating, whether asleep, conscious or unconscious. If you, for example, let your hand be gently massaged, you say that this is pleasing to your hand. It is the hand that feels this pleasure. In this sense, you can say your hand has an "I." If you say that your hand has free will and you have a loving relationship with your hand, the free will of your hand becomes a love affair between you and your hand. It develops into a fine instrument that serves the whole body, mind and soul. It works impeccably and lovingly together with your other hand, legs, feet and mind. This goes for all your organs, and you can actually talk to all your organs, and they constantly give you feedback. Cold feet and hangovers included. Each and every one of your cells has consciousness, and just as you are cells of Great Spirit or God/dess or "the Whole," and just as you are fed and nourished by me, the Earth, your hand is fed by the rest of your body and your hands serve the rest of your body, too. In this sense it is all one.

But to continue to answer how you create reality….

Earth:

*Whenever you have true desire
and the belief that the desire can be fulfilled,
it can.*

Holding an intent, which may or may not be translated into images or thoughts, is closely entwined with perception. Physics has recognized the "observer effect"[7] at a small scale. Now it is up to you to recognize it and put it to use at a large scale.

One of the first steps towards creating or co-creating reality consciously consists of taking charge of what goes on in your head. This begins by becoming aware of what goes on in your head. After that comes the realization that it is possible to change or control what you are doing in your head. Yet another level of discernment has to do with finding what it is that you desire, beyond the fairly superficial desires that others, for example and for their own reasons, want you to have. Here, your bodies provide excellent feedback.

What I am therefore suggesting is that you start becoming aware of what you intend.[8] Only then can you recognize the correlation between your intent and the reality that presents itself. Parts of your society call this the power of prayer, yet it does not require any God to whom one directs the prayer. Others simply deny the possibility of influencing reality without actively intervening physically.

When humans do not create their reality consciously, their reality is on automatic. This means that they do not question their beliefs, their patterns, their past or what they are doing. It is like being stuck in first grade, forgetting that after first grade comes second grade. This is nothing that should be forced, for old patterns ultimately either

---

7 In science, the term "observer effect" means that the act of observing will influence the phenomenon being observed.

8 To "intend" is here used as an active verb, something you do with your mind, not simply a statement of a wish.

die, providing mulch for the new, or they transform, awakening new possibilities. The decision to not leave one's comfort zone, to remain in one's old patterns, often opening the door for slow decay and ultimate death, does not mean that you are less loved or that you are less important. It simply means that you are choosing that path for yourself. You are using your freedom to explore that avenue. And yet I, the Earth, for one, am knocking at your door, asking you to let me in, holding out a hand of heartfelt cooperation. When you go to a new country, it takes time before you get to know the weather, the people, the landscape, the food, the fruits, the language, the clothes and the modes of communication. In my terms you are recent arrivals. Early man was fairly quick to align with me and get to know me at a certain level – more as spontaneous children than as an adult partner. Your turning away from your connection with the Earth can be seen as a rebellion during puberty. It is only when we see ourselves as separate that we can blame each other, and true understanding can only come from deep communion. When subconscious or unconscious processes become conscious, the totality is more encompassing and thus more relevant when it comes to creating reality; for when you co-create or create individually, it is your whole being that is creating, not just the conscious or the subconscious part. There is no part of you that is not participating in the creation of your reality.

As I have said before, when we are deeply connected I act as an incubator for your thoughts and desires. This is why I suggest that you connect with me in your everyday life.

> *Earth:*
>
> *Many people have reported
> that at the height of lovemaking
> they cannot tell who is doing what,
> and that they act as one being together.*
>
> *That is the level of unity that is operating
> when it comes to consciously co-creating reality.*

When it comes to this book, it is not a question of me telling you, Sten, what to write. When you ask a question of me, either from you or from someone else, the answer is created together with that question. When I answer it, all I do is add my energies, just as you add yours when you ask a question. It is not that I "know" everything; it is just that the answer arises in me as the question is asked. This means, of course, that those asking these questions are co-creating the answers, together with me, for we are not as separate as it sometimes may seem. We are truly co-creating this book. Not because you are writing and I am talking, but because it is a joint process that is happening in terms of the content as well.

Individual and collective

Earth: When it comes to co-creation, you could equally follow the reality and thoughts of an individual and they will ultimately lead to the same view, for with time the individual expands to become a larger unit who is in connection and cooperation with the whole, erasing the boundaries, redefining the individual as not only a part of the whole, but ultimately *as* the whole, the non-exclusive whole.

Individuality and collectiveness are two facets of the same reality. The way you use your attention to focus on one or the other, or the interconnection between them, determines the color or characteristics or feeling of the reality you create. In relation to this book, this means that the creation, the writing of this book changes, affects and constitutes a transformation of the author; of me, the Earth; and of you, the reader. As I have said, every creation transforms its creator. This goes for an artist, for what you call God, for me, the Earth, and for you.

This book is a joint effort between me, you, the people who have asked questions and the reader. But the fact that the reader is a co-creator of this book, as it is being read, might not be understood quite yet.

Sten: Can you say more about the reader co-creating this book?

Earth: Yes, it has to do with the resonance of thought. Thoughts resonate across time. When a reader picks up a thought, he or she is co-creating. When a reader resonates with a thought, the resonance goes both ways and through time. You are usually not aware of rapid changes in reality because you step seamlessly into the new reality which is then provided with a whole new past. And this is going on constantly. This means that you are not so much changing your past as choosing a different reality that comes with a corresponding past. However, these processes are slightly more complex than that.

Befriending the Unknown

Sten: From our three-dimensional view, how can thoughts affect large-scale reality?

Earth: Your image of creation always involves going in and changing something. This requires effort. Original creation is effortless. As I mentioned, the process involved is not so much one of changing reality as one of choosing reality. What you see as "cause and effect" is nothing more than the choice of a reality that conforms to rules you have collectively chosen. Again, these processes are so quick and so engrained that you do not notice them. But from a certain perspective, what you are doing is pure magic. It is, however, seldom conscious magic; but it will become so.

Understanding your relationship with the outer three-dimensional world, learning to control it, and realizing that controlling it is not necessarily what you want, is just one step of your learning to both take your power and align yourself with the "greater." Total control equals death. This is nothing bad, for it clears the way for new creation. As you change your view of yourself, from being an individual human being, into being a consciousness that can tune into any other thing or consciousness, your desires change. You no longer see control as the best way to impact reality, for in essence it does not conform to your deepest desire – just as you do not wish to control someone you love deeply. When you use your innate powers of creation, the desire to control is replaced by an often playful and artistic approach to your own life. When you see your life as a piece of art and you become the brush that bridges between you and your life, you become the joyful tool, the tool that takes joy in creating the work of art that is you.

From one perspective the future is creating the now. This means that in a sense you are creating your parents. The arrow of time has one direction and another virtual opposite one, which means that your relationship to the past is a creative one and not a passive cause-effect relationship. So you are already connected with your future, with you in the future. This future you is always knocking or scratching on the door of your consciousness.

Whenever you are surprised, there is an opening in your consciousness. Lowering your guard and letting in the unknown is something you can also do at will through intent. Already the thought of letting the unknown enter your body and expand into your heart-space connects you with the flow that resonates with the you in the future, for it is flows – three-dimensional flows of a certain kind within you, in your present reality – that automatically resonate with similar flows throughout and through time, i.e. at what you would call different times. From the perspective of these flows themselves, time becomes the different scenes of a movie, of the movies of your lives. And seen in greater detail, they become the individual photos that make up the movie reels of your reality. One of the most powerful ways to open this channel through time is by using the energies of heartfelt sexuality. You can thereby become the one who scratches at the door of the future you, and it is when the two scratchers harmonize and recognize each other as one that the greater transpersonal and trans-time being becomes the one you recognize as yourself, as your true transpersonal self.

There are thoughts that can engender feelings that have an impact on your entire energetic system. An example: When you have had serious difficulties of any kind and have succeeded in overcoming them, you often experience a great sense of relief, resulting in what one could call "relaxing into having overcome." Such feelings can also be engendered without any "cause." In this sense, you are much freer to create your emotional state of being than you are usually aware of. When engaged in the creation of such positive emotions and thoughts, you are co-creating not only yourself, but your entire environment, for you are radiating new patterns with which other parts of reality are in resonance.

The idea that a lack of awareness and consciousness simply needs to be let go of must also be translated into new habits. In a sense this is like allowing bowel movements, which is a process of letting go, but is nevertheless sometimes done with much effort and pushing, even pain. Learning instead to relax, open up and let go is a process that resonates with what we do when we let go of rigid ideas and beliefs. But these new habits are different for everyone and there is no limit to the creativity that is yours to be expressed here.

Earth:

*Separation always leads to union,
and just as an in-breath always leads to an out-breath,
union always scatters the seeds of union to the winds.*

Chapter 2. Co-thinking

A Family of One

Earth: One of the pillars of this book has to do with a vision of what happens when we join together and act as one. Once we have that view, we can see ourselves as different parts of one family: One being, where one hand knows what the other is doing. This means aligning our agendas or our motives with that of the other, so as to create a joint agenda, with both of us seeing the world from that agenda or point of view. This will open up new vistas, because we will not see our job as being how to help the Earth or how to help the human being. But we will also not see it as if the Earth and the human being have always been one, for they have not. **We are coming together to create a family of one.** At the heart of this cooperative one-ness lies love and kinship. And in a sense we have come together to procreate a child which is nothing less than a new world.

> *"Another world is not only possible,
> she is on her way.*
>
> *On a quiet day
> I can hear her breathing."*
>
> Arundhati Roy, Indian author and activist

When in a family the mother, for example, makes a decision, she is making a decision for the entire family, which includes herself. She knows of her own importance, for together with the father she needs to be the decision-maker and designer of the life of the family. And she does not make decisions regarding herself at the cost of the others.

This co-thinking is not just another way of thinking; it is something that attracts us because it is very much who we are.

From "We" to a new "I"

But we need to take this one step further. Much has been written about "thinking as 'we,'" and it does represent a step away from a more limited view of who we are. But who is this "we"? As long as it remains a plural "we," it constitutes an addition, not a unit.

Earth: I want you to think about the "we" as an "I." This gives rise to thoughts that later can be seen affecting its different parts. This thinking "as I" is a way of expanding your individuality, finding a greater self-image than your regular "I."

Difficulties

I found this to be exceptionally difficult, but also exciting. I had known of the idea of thinking as "we" as a spiritual practice, for example, when meditating together with others and aligning with the "We-field." I could also fairly easily imagine or "feel" what it was like to align myself with the Earth and think "with the Earth," especially after all the communications I had had with her before. Switching to the idea that this "we" exists as an "I" that I can, so to speak, "become" was an adventure of the mind in and of itself. I was then no longer "I," nor was I "I with the Earth." Instead, it was as if the inner boundaries of my regular "I" were dissolved and I expanded greatly. Yet it was difficult for me to gain any new insights from this state.

Sten: Earth, I'm trying to grok what it really means to look at things from the perspective of Earth plus me as an "I." I'm trying to sense this as different from my normal state of being, yet I do not feel this changes what I perceive or think. But I can sense an expanded feeling. Can this state of being connected, as I experience being one with the Earth, become stable and productive?

Earth: No, it is not productive. You are still giving away too much of yourself. You are retrogressing instead of progressing.

You are again becoming a child of the Earth by becoming symbiotic with the Earth, becoming one with the Earth. This is not what is meant. This is why you do not get any new thoughts.

Sten: OK, I would like to experience the power that lies in thinking together with the Earth as one "I." Can you provide me with an example or experience of this?

Earth: I cannot provide you with an experience, but I can experience it with you. As you rightly say, when we go into this experience, we expand. This experience of expansion is not immediate or full, and you are yourself grappling with what it means and what it feels like. There are many things holding you back from letting go of your feeling of an individualized "I" that is limited to your own self and body. But this is only by force of habit. Other cultures have experienced entirely different senses of self, which have included a union with their tribe or with their surroundings at a much deeper level than what you are used to. Yet even being a fan of a football team is a small step in this direction. When you create a family and become a mother or father, you also shift identities. The more you expand your sense of self, the more power you attain. Power here means ability to do.

Sten: How does this change my thinking?

Earth: It is not your thinking that changes. It is the thinker who changes. What especially changes is your ability to tune in to the different parts of the greater "I." When you become the "I" of the Earth and you, you start to feel the Earth in your body. Taken deeply, this can lead to many things, such as insights about the growth processes and needs of plants. It can teach you to align with the weather. It can let you see the connections in nature more deeply, between animals, plants, the earth, water, the air. But it can also give you insights about many other things, such as how to deal with your so-called "trash," cleaning up the oceans, gaining energy out of what you call "nothing," improving nutrition by working together with plants, transforming chemical elements as a path toward creating anything out of anything. Ultimately, any of your issues can gain immensely through the awakening of this new "I." And I, too, will gain greatly, for I will be able to hold thoughts that I could not access on my own. As with all your faculties, accessing and "feeding" this new "I" also needs to be trained.

Our true "I"

Earth: The determiner within you, the true "I," is the one who decides what form to take. The normal form you take when you determine who you are as separate from all others and everything around you, is simply a determination made by the deeper "I" to explore the world from that point of view.

The determiner within you is the one who takes true pleasure in shifting between the various identifications of the "I." You can reach this state of pleasure automatically when you are making love, for that expands your sense of self to encompass more. But it not only gives you pleasure and grows your love, it also gives you knowledge. Expanding your "I" to include the other gives you entirely new perspectives, allowing for a symbiosis of knowledge that is greater than the knowledge of the sum of its parts. Your computer specialists are aware of this when they connect several computers with each other into arrays of computers. In a sense, a greater being is thus created that is able to do things of an entirely different order. Creating such networks of computers also changes the people who connect the networks.

So what is this new "I" like?

Earth: When the Earth and a human connect with each other in this way, a third arises. This is the two of them together as one. Both of them, individually, have access to this "one." At the same time, when they both become this co-thinking and co-being being, this third exists within each of them. It is in this third entity that communication occurs. In its essence, communication is an event – one event. It is not a back and forth. It may take the expression of back and forth, but the actual communication is always an occurrence within the unit of the two as one. It is when we choose the perspective of individuality that communication expresses itself as a back and forth process. Yet even in this back and forth process, the actual communication is within the two as one being, although this to you is then stretched out through time.

The purest form of communication as one is the joint orgasm of the unit that comes about through the union of the male and the female.[9] This orgasm is very different from the female orgasm or the male orgasm, although it incorporates both. Yet the combination of both yields a third which lies at the heart of existence, at the heart of every atom, at the heart of every galaxy. Thus orgasm is not so much an event as a dynamic state underlying all of creation. It is the natural state of all of reality. And all of reality is engaged in evolution.

---

9 This refers to the male and female principles, the interactions between the male and female energy flows, and has nothing to do with sexual preferences.

Blue moon

It was three in the morning, the first of August, and this night there was a so-called blue moon, meaning there were two full moons in the month of July. I got up to go to the bathroom and looked out the window. I saw the moon outside and thought: "This would be a really good time to go outside and attempt to talk to the Earth, to see what new thoughts might come up." But I was dead tired, so I returned to bed, thinking: "Just let me lie down a bit and I'll think about it." In bed, I thought I really should get up, but… my eyelids were so heavy, and it was like fighting against something very, very strong. After a while I thought about getting up again, but it was exactly the same.

I then remembered how the Earth had asked me to think in terms of "we" and become, in a sense, "Earth and I" as yet another "I." I was wondering how that really translates and what I see then that is different from what I usually see, for I hadn't managed to do that before. So I put myself into that space, as best I could, and then again I thought about getting up. Suddenly, it was as if any and all resistance had vanished. It was like: "Yes, of course, what a wonderful idea to get up now." I threw the covers aside and got up, totally amazed at my own transformation. This was the first time I had an experience of my own of what it might mean to think as a "we" that has become an "I."

Sten: Earth, I would love to see the practical applications of thinking as one. I have experienced it briefly when I got up during the blue moon, but I would like to see it applied in other areas.

Earth: That is what your questions are here for. They are not here for me to answer individually; they are here to show you and others the enormous possibilities created by humans aligning with the Earth and vice versa. Part of what is keeping you from doing this naturally is a fear that comes from not knowing my motives, because you are not aware of them. So one goal of these books is to let you feel and understand my motives from within.

The basic quality needed here is one of trust. For humans to think of "we," the Earth and humans, in terms of an "I" means no longer seeing life as a fight. It also means getting to know one another from within.

Trust

(Excerpt from the book *I Am With You*.)

You have forgotten the determinative quality of trusting.

Trusting is not the passive quality of letting happen what happens.

It is taking responsibility for what happens by exuding, insisting on, being received.

From this state of being, the way you attract thoughts regarding a certain issue is different from the way you have done it as an individual "I." You, as an individual consciousness, are now accessing the consciousness of the greater "I," the Human-Earth "I." Again, imagine the human being energetically making love and fusing with me, the Earth.

***

The image I got was of the human being and the Earth, twirling as one around the Sun; and through our connection, we, as a unit, were pulsating.

***

Earth: This is an energetic pulsing that we are an integral part of. Again, it is not the Earth pulsing, and we[10] pulsing with it; nor is it we pulsing and the Earth pulsing with us. It is pulsing as one unit, as a unit with consciousness. We are awakening the Earth-Human consciousness as one being that we can access at will. It comes about through the union of our life forces through lovemaking in its widest sense.

Looking at the Human-Earth system, there is a disconnect within it, between humans and the Earth that are parts of this system – the key being that this is occurring within one system, within one being. So what needs to be healed is not the human being, nor the Earth itself, nor the relationship between the human being and the Earth. It is the Human-Earth being that needs to be healed.

---

10 This is a typical example of how, as mentioned in the Introduction, in my communication the perspective sometimes changed from that of the Earth to that of a "we," referring to human beings.

There is a trauma within this system, this being.

Take the issues of tsunamis or global warming. Were we to look at these in a judgmental way and in a separation-type of perspective – and all judgment is based on non-union, on separation, on not understanding the whole – then we could blame the Earth for giving us tsunamis and earthquakes, or blame the human being for exploiting the Earth as a dead thing, burning coal and oil at breakneck speed, building where it is known that it is dangerous to live, etc. But this is a very limited view, a view based on separation, and any understanding of a relationship needs to be based on an understanding of the whole, the union, the unified being of both.

This understanding leads to an absence of judgment, not based on any kind of forgiveness or special benevolence, but based on the one you become when the judge and the judged recognize each other as being one and the same. It automatically leads to a change in behavior, which is no longer a change of one or the other, but of the being that has recognized itself as one.

The quality of this union is the same as that which can be reached through lovemaking. It is also the same as the union between a mother and its child in the womb, when they are as one.

> *Earth:*
>
> *But the goal is not to become one with the Earth;*
> *it is to go back and forth*
> *between thinking, feeling and acting as one,*
> *and thinking, feeling and acting as an individual.*

It is the whole system that is feeling the pain of separation. This is a part of the entire "rendering asunder," the split that goes through Creation and life. There was a rendering asunder for the native Americans when the white man came to America. Even being born, which should be a beautiful, loving, sexy, painless process, is a rendering asunder, as is the entire process around aging and dying, which in reality means regaining that great union – the beautiful gaining of peace by breathing out.

If you apply this thinking to other areas, a pattern will become visible that makes sense to you. If we take the issue of ISIS, the Islamic State – and one of the questioners was asking how we can learn to deal with ISIS – it is only by seeing the activities and thinking of ISIS as connected to what the rest of humanity is doing that you can understand and learn to deal with it. If you wish to understand the root cause of ISIS, trace it back to its beginnings and find within yourself the corresponding impulse, striving or vision that brought forth this movement. By finding the essence – and the essence is always one that is shared by all of humanity – one can see what kind of suppression has led to the rising of ISIS, what non-fulfillment it is an expression of.

It is always by becoming one and at the same time allowing multitude that true insight is gained. When you are connected to this larger picture, you are harmonizing with higher levels, and this will bring you new experiences and new thoughts. You can relax into it, and this relaxation brings the newness of a new day. Practicing this every day would be very productive. The relaxation you feel will drop down into the steady gaining of insights. These insights are not like answers to questions; they are questions and answers at the same time.

Sten: But how does this sense of one-ness relate to individuality?

Earth: An ant colony operates as one. It also sends out scouts, searching for food – just like Lewis and Clark. As Lewis and Clark were on their own out in the wild, engaged in reconnaissance and discovery, they were doing this for society at large. And yet they had made the individual decision to go on the trek and how to deal with each and every situation they met. It was a free will expedition. The same is true in this case; the individual and the collective simply represent different perspectives.

***

I was still unsatisfied with my attempts to think or see the world from the perspective of this new "I," so as I was finishing writing this book, again out in the desert of Arizona, I decided to try it again, out in nature. As I did so, as best I could, I again felt expanded, and I wandered around in the desert. I came to a large bush and looked at it, thinking that I was, in a sense, looking at myself, for the Earth had brought forth this bush and the Earth was a part of me. So, somewhat flippantly, but totally seriously, I said, "Good evening, bush." Something clicked, and when I looked around it was as if all the bushes and cactuses were little beings that had come alive and were relating to me.

As I continued to walk, I thought back to an email I had received that morning, asking me to contribute to the cause of stopping the poaching of elephants in Africa. Recently 600 elephants had been killed for their ivory tusks in a National Park in Cameroon. There was a photo of several elephants that had had their faces hacked off to get at the tusks. The article said that four elephants are killed every hour and at this rate they would soon be extinct. I have always felt a deep kinship with elephants and decided to contribute to those fighting this poaching by donating $50. But in my present state of tentatively experiencing this new "I," the thought of that photo triggered a powerful reaction in me. It was as if I simply had to do something much more powerful than just sending money. I had to act as if it depended on me to stop this slaughter, taking into full consideration the widest-ranging associated issues, since I was well aware of the fact that there was much more involved than just stopping the poachers. But the main thing was that it felt as if I had hurt a part of my body and I had to do something about it. I took a stand for it. That was when it dawned on me: Yes, it wasn't my thinking that had changed; it was I, the thinker, who had changed. I now encompassed elephants at a much deeper level than before.

Chapter 3. Co-Visioning

Vision

Earth: When humans for the first time put a seed in the Earth, it changed the direction of evolution, because humans became co-creators at a whole new level. This was the materialization of the ability to imagine, for imagination is putting the seed of a future reality into the womb of the thought field[11] of today.

This is called "vision," for it is closely related to seeing. We often regard seeing as becoming aware of or making an image, a true image, like a photograph, of a reality that exists independently of us. We say this in part because when we ask others, they see more or less the same thing, as far as we can

---

11 The existence of such a thought field has been proposed by the Jesuit theologian Teilhard de Chardin. He called it the "noosphere."

determine. So if we have found a way of "looking at reality" in such a way that we agree on what we see, we regard that as "objective" and not subjective. Actually, it is collectively subjective. What we see is a function of how we relate to the outer world. Were we to relate differently, by touching it differently, what we would see would be very different; we would "assemble" the outer world differently.

Actually, I am bringing forth or birthing the best in the human being and the human being is bringing forth the best in me, the Earth. We are truly birthing each other. So even as the human being is exploring Pluto, and ultimately even other stars within our galaxy and other galaxies, this is all part of the intimate coming together in conscious marriage of the Earth and humans. Just as I, the Earth, can feel and understand what humans are doing among themselves, so will you be able to understand what I am doing with other planets. It is when we connect consciously with each other at a deeper and deeper level that I can take you on journeys, opening portals for you to go on journeys to other stars, planets and galaxies, and discover the exciting possibilities that lie in what you call time warps, other dimensions and other universes. But let us get closer to home.

Vision is creating from the future. Whenever we enter into resonance with what we desire – whenever we create vision – we are establishing a line of intent between now and a future where that desire is fulfilled. This is like defining a seed.

> At one point during these conversations I said to the Earth: "You have to help me here; this is not easy."
>
> The answer I got was: "No, you have to help yourself from your own future. Set the intent of the book by sensing its power and allow it to pull you from the future."
>
> Quite a challenge…

Vision has to do not only with seeing, but also with seeking. A thirsty person seeks water. The saying that "not only does a thirsty person seek water, but the water seeks the thirsty person" is a reflection of the fact that Creation and Creator[12] are interchangeable. Creation in the service of its Creator is identical with the Creator being in the service of his/her Creation. Being of service to one's servant engenders love at a very deep level.

---

[12] The term "Creator" should here more accurately be the cumbersome "Creator/Creatrix."

> *Earth:*
>
> *All of Creation is a work of art,*
> *and every work of art creates the artist,*
> *forms the artist.*
>
> *When you realize that Creation*
> *is as sacred as the Creator/Creatrix,*
> *you will be in awe of and fall in love with*
> *all of Creation that surrounds you —*
> *with the streets of Cleveland,*
> *as well as with your bathroom walls,*
> *and with your friends*
> *and your so-called enemies alike.*

The visioning I am talking about is not just imagination, much less fantasy. It is more like informing your own cells of the reality of a desired vision. It begins by loosening the fixation on what is, recognizing it as ultimately a specific way of choosing to see reality in a certain way. Visioning is one of the most powerful and elementary ways of designing or creating reality.

Many things that you do are not based on conscious present-time decisions. They are an automatic result of decisions that have been made before. When you go walking, you do not make a conscious decision every time to lift one foot and place it in front of the other one. You have made a decision to go some place, and this decision carries you forward. The same is true for many of my own activities. They then also lead to things like earthquakes, volcanoes, etc. I cannot stop those any more than you can stop the blood flowing in your veins. And yet we both act consciously.

Co-visioning

What we want to do and what is needed is for us to create joint vision.

Visioning is not simply an act; it is also a state of being. It is a state of connectedness with a chosen future that is constantly revealing itself anew. When you become friends with the future, the future reveals itself like a shy young woman, often in surprising ways. If you instead approach the future as a threat and a source of panic, you will tend to awaken a corresponding possible future for yourself.

Co-visioning, or co-envisioning, with me is done by the "I" that is the union of both you and me. When you "separate" them back, they are no longer this "I." When co-visioning, this joint "I" opens up to a future that is based on its own vibration. The vibration of this larger "I" is much more powerful and has a much greater effect than those of the "I" of humans and the "I" of the Earth.

The greater trust, love and presence that is a quality of this larger "I" radiates to attract a future that is in resonance with it. Being held by the Earth, holding the Earth, being one with the Earth, serving the Earth and tending to the Earth are expressions of this unity, expressed through independent, individualized acts.

Now that your economic systems are experiencing major difficulties because they are not in harmony with the laws of your own nature, and changes are occurring on Earth in terms not only of climate but also of my magnetic field and my many other subtle energies that your scientists have become increasingly aware of – and this includes the finer aspects of Northern and Southern lights that you interact with – it is becoming crucial for you to allow me into your consciousness so that you can see and understand how I am and have always been interacting with you. This is a part of you that is insisting and desiring to become consciously known, both individually and by humanity as a whole. It is a process of self-healing of the human being and of me, the Earth, and it is occurring right now. Seen from this perspective, you are discovering what can rightly be called the light in the darkness.

If we look at global warming, the question is not if this is human-caused or not. The question is much more: Do you act on the beliefs that you truly have? If you do not act in some way, you are like a fish that has decided not to swim. You are and have been designed as thinkers, as actors, as doers, as lovers, as emotionally alive beings. To the extent that you have had experiences that have blocked you, made you complacent or bitter, that have made you retreat into your purely personal thoughts and agendas without opening up to the world around you, a deeper part of you that is still intact will push you from within, either to die and start over or to push through until it reaches your consciousness. This is how you have designed yourself to function. It is still true that if you find more attractive ways of designing how you function, then that will increasingly become true. For example, if you focus on having positive surprises without the feeling that you need to earn them, if you open yourself up to positive surprises, this can increasingly become a part of your reality.

> *Sten:*
>
> *Imagine a "positive 9/11."*
>
> *This is a positive event, discovery or shift that is at least as powerful in its effect as 9/11.*
>
> *It changes everything and irreversibly opens up a bright future.*

Sten: What is the difference between co-thinking and co-visioning?

Earth: Co-thinking is what you are doing now. You are connecting with me, as one "I." You have a question, and you open up and see what comes, what thoughts come. It can also occur without questions – a flow of thinking, a change in perspective that opens up new thoughts.

Visioning is when you start with something that you like – or an idea or an image or a desire – you throw it out into the future, and you reel in the line. When you do this, matter attaches to the line, just as when you throw out a fishing line in the ocean and let it lie for a while. You then get all kinds of mussels and crabs hanging on to the line, based on what was in that direction. This is in a sense what is happening when you vision.

Co-visioning with me is when you and I do this as the "I" consisting of me and you as one. By doing this you will learn much about the Earth, for you are doing this from a state of connection with a being whose processes and intent you are only slowly getting to know consciously.

Nothing exists as separate from the whole. So if you, for example, want to see yourself through the eyes of the Earth, this can only be done from the embeddedness of you within the rest. The Earth can only see you as a part of itself, and you can only see the Earth as a part of yourself, of the larger system of "I plus the Earth," of the "We," of the greater "I" that encompasses the two. This is always what happens when something "sees" something else. We cannot see ourselves through our own eyes. Every attempt to do so will always be skewed. We can only see ourselves through the compounded eyes of ourselves and someone else.

Chapter 4. Equity

Same, same, but different

Right from the beginning, the Earth wanted me to include a chapter about "Equity" in this book. Having mainly heard of the term "equity" in connection with "equity capital," or in the word "equitable," I was not aware of its precise meaning or what the Earth meant when using the word. As usual, when trying to get a new concept across, the Earth used analogies to explain what she meant by equity, beginning with an analogy regarding size….

Earth: Size is something very relative. If you have a large object and a small object, there is a point between the two where, if looked at from that point, they both look equally large or where their effect is equal. An example of this is that although the Sun is much larger than the Moon, from Earth they look approximately the same size. Another example is the so-called Lagrange point, a point in space between the Earth and the Sun where the gravitational pull of the Earth is equal to that of the Sun. A satellite suspended at this point will not fall to Earth nor will it move toward the Sun. Instead it will follow the Earth around the Sun, always "seeing" the sunlit part of Earth.

Analogously, this means that if you take any two things in the Universe, they can communicate with each other from a perspective where they are "as equals;" they can communicate as equals. Move that point of reference closer to the smaller one, and the smaller one dominates, and vice versa.

This means that there is a certain point of view where the smallest grain of sand is, in a sense, "equal to" the largest galaxy. From a certain perspective, every part of the Universe is "equal." Yet we are free to choose our perspective, giving more importance to anything. From the perspective of the whole, the question then becomes not what is most important, but what is the relationship or "distance" between two things that best benefits both and thus the whole?

Hordes of friends

At one point during my communion with the Earth, when I was feeling very open and deeply connected with my surroundings, I heard a bird fluttering and looked up. It was standing still, fluttering in the air. Suddenly it started to move. I followed it intently as it flew toward the Sun, imagining I was the bird. Just as it crossed the Sun, I was blinded and could not see it, but on the other side of the Sun I picked it up again, or at least what I was sure was the bird. In reality it was something much closer; it was a bumblebee flying a few feet in front of me, but my attention had already shifted to it, believing it was the bird. This was an amazing experience which felt as if I had shifted who I am, for I had connected so deeply with the bird. Suddenly "being" the bumblebee showed me that my awareness can go without effort from the large to the small, from the far away to the near and remain in the same feeling of awe of the natural world. It felt as if the bird was calling out for attention, and I gave it my full attention, which I also kept as it suddenly (from my perspective) transformed into a bumblebee.

Another thing I learned, at least tentatively, is that when I enter into that state of union, of an enlarged "I," which encompasses the Earth and my "regular I," I open myself up to miracles and wonders of perception, awareness and magic. The door opens and you can start talking to your

> surroundings. I closed in on that possibility and that reality, and as I did so, tears came to my eyes, for I was sensing the approaching of hordes of friends.

Equity is not equality. When human beings experience pain and sorrow caused by human actions and emotions, they often try to overcome this by instituting a kind of equality or a kind of union that does not allow for differences. Equity, on the other hand, is more related to freedom, expressed as differences. Fear and equity are opposites. When there is little equity, fear increases; for when there is no equity, there is nowhere else to go. You are stuck within a definition of who you are and your situation, allowing for little change. In a sense it is also wrong to say that we are all equally important and thus require the same attention. Importance is chosen. Equity is given. It is not always necessary to focus on what is important. Beauty, for example, is something that does not define itself in terms of importance.

When the seed of a tree is placed in the ground, it sends out roots and it grows upward. The leaves receive light from the Sun and they open up to create a large surface area, lifting their faces to the Sun. But the tree is doing more than that. It is exhibiting itself. It is showing its inner beauty to the world. If you allow yourself the thought that every tree is exhibiting its beauty **to you,** you begin to enter into a living relationship with nature, in which your appreciation and emotional reaction is felt by your surroundings. The same is true for me, the Earth.

The river of inner knowing

I went down to the lake below the house I was staying in as I wrote this book and connected with the Earth.

Earth: From this place here, sitting at the water, in the morning with the full blue moon, you have access to more subconscious levels than otherwise. From here we can talk about what we call equity. How the small and the large are equal. How a child and an old person should be listened to with equal presence as youths or adults. A baby can teach you more about your own life than you think is possible.

There is a river of inner knowing that flows through your life from beginning to end. When you access this inner knowing, you can get answers to questions you did not even know you had, but that have been guiding your life. All questions you have can be related to this inner knowing.

The baby might say to the adult: "You are searching for answers at the surface of life. Instead, come, be where the answers are." For the symbiosis between the question and the answer is such that it is equally valid to say that the answer has given rise to the question. A truth is trying to come out, and it does this by awakening a question in you. This will not be easy for you to understand, for you are not used to being with the answer, being where the answer is.

Equity is the oil that makes things harmonious. It is the absence of judgment that comes from oneness. It is what makes it possible to move one's attention from one thing to another, thereby gaining energy, for the overall system is more than equal. It is built on dynamic growth, and when you are aligned with dynamic growth or development – which might well include the opposite of growth, disintegration – there is a natural course for your attention to take toward greater knowledge, wisdom, pleasure and magic.

Equity among humans is what allows for a greater intimacy and vice versa. And intimacy creates equity. When intimacy with another reaches a certain level, they become interchangeable. This is what is meant by equity here. If we were to have an accident – for example, slip and fall down and hurt ourselves – we would never think of blaming a part of our body, such as our foot or one of our eyes, and then try to punish it. That would be absurd. Nobody would deny the difference between a hand and a foot, yet nobody would declare that either one of them is not an integral part of their body and of lesser inherent value than the other. This is what is meant when it is sometimes said, "You are all God's children." Applied to the Human/Earth system, it means that all the emotions, thoughts and energies of the Earth are fully accessible to the human being, no matter how different we are. For this level of equity and intimacy to occur between humans and Earth, new experiences are needed. These are inner experiences that may then be reflected outward. Their quality is not one of proof. It is more a question of a knowing becoming manifest; for both knowing and manifestation of that knowing are parts of a whole, of one process.

To get this process going a seeming "leap of faith" is required. It is an inner process whereby a felt possibility is combined with a desired outcome. First of all, to see if a telephone works, or if there is somebody at the other end, you need to speak into it. Then you need to listen. Any proof can be disproved, but no action can be disproved. The desire shows the direction; the belief in the possibility opens the door.

Tat Tvam Asi[13]

One day, sitting down at the lake, I looked out at the great, majestic splendor of nature, and I connected with the Earth.

Earth: Look at this greatness and this vastness. This is you.

When I heard those words, it was as if the entire landscape and lake I was standing in front of (practically on, for I was on a pontoon) opened up *within* me. In fact, a whole Universe opened up within me. Yet another part of me, the one who was standing at the cusp between looking out and looking in, the one looking, felt alone, wanted someone to share the experience with and needed to be redeemed. It was the one that was seeking the eyes and the hands of another and at the same time seeking to crawl into creation and become as natural as the beautiful blade of a reed bending in the wind, reflecting the sunlight. Or the dragonfly that stood vibrating in front of me, looking at me, then taking off to court a lady dragonfly close by. To me, this

---

13 "Tat tvam asi" is a Sanskrit phrase, which means "Thou art that," saying that the Self – in its original, pure state – is identical with the Ultimate Reality that is the ground and origin of all phenomena.

desire to become an effortless, natural part of an alive world with the dazzling natural motions of a dragonfly or the perfection and beauty in a stalk of reed, reminded me of when Dylan sings: "I want to dance beneath the diamond sky, with one hand waving free, silhouetted by the sea …".

Sten: Earth, I am going through inner movements through what we are talking about, movements that open up my heart and surge and tug at it.

Earth: Yes, that is what we are all about. Those surges and tugs reverberate throughout the Universe. Can you imagine a molecule feeling?

Dewdrops

Sten: Earth, I have a question. It arose through how I've seen nature out here; how in the mornings, right at the top of the blades of grass, there is often a drop of dew, and when the rays of the Sun hits those drops, it is dazzling. This is something that Viktor Schauberger, an Austrian unorthodox naturalist and inventor, has written about, saying that these are very special drops. Can you tell me something about this?

Earth: Look at what is happening. The Sun touches the water that has coalesced from the air and is hanging in midair from a stalk of grass. I call this the rainbow bridge from Earth to Sun. It has a newness about it and although it keeps happening every day, or at least every day when the dew forms and the Sun comes through, yet it is a sign of the true newness of the first time, of the miracle of birth and of the power of beauty. It is true that these drops are extremely valuable, for they can trigger within you the possibility of new worlds and the rejuvenation of your whole being. So before you ask, can I put them to use, for example, within medicine, within healing or within agriculture, let them impact your soul, let them inside, with light and all, and start to feel what it means to be them.

This is deeply related to the first rays of the Sun, the miracle of a new day, of the newly born, the releasing into the wild of wild animals, the general amnesty given by the stroke of a pen and the first minutes or hours when school is over and summer break begins.

It is true that something remarkable happens in that little drop of water, but it is not something that you can simply collect in a bucket and use as an elixir. For as soon as you collect the drops, the magic disappears. And yet they drive you on, they spur you on, eliciting hope again, and again, and again. Understanding the principle involved makes it possible for you to harness this principle for many purposes. It has to do with the delicate balance of a drop of water suffused by the rays of the Sun. Beauty awakened. Beauty kissed to life. As you know, light can heal, and it is the light from this droplet that impacts your soul so strongly. Your angels and your fairies are real, and they can teach you much about the bridge between light and matter.

Identifying with nature

(An excerpt from the book The Nature of the Psyche *by Jane Roberts, speaking for Seth, her trance personality, about the sense of self of early man on Earth.)*

Speaking historically [...] man first identified with nature, and loved it, for he saw it as an extension of himself even while he felt himself a part of its expression. In exploring it he explored himself also.

———

Generally, you experience the self as isolated from nature, and primarily enclosed within your skin. Early man did not feel like an empty shell, and yet selfhood existed for him as much ***outside*** of the body as within it. There was a constant interaction. It is easy to say to you that such people could identify, say, with the trees, but an entirely different thing to try to explain what it would be like for a mother to become so a part of the tree underneath which her children played that she could keep track of them ***from the tree's viewpoint***, though she was herself far away.

———

To explore the exterior world was to explore the inner one. Such a person, however, walking through the forest, also felt that he or she was also a portion of the inner life of each rock or tree, materialized. Yet there was no contradiction of identities.

A man might merge his own consciousness with a running stream, traveling in such a way for miles to explore the layout of the land. To do this he became part water in a kind of identification you can barely understand – but so did the water then become part of the man.

From the book The Nature of Personal Reality © 1974, Jane Roberts. Reprinted by permission of Amber-Allen Publishing, www.amberallen.com, San Rafael, CA 94903. All rights reserved.

Earth: When you start listening to me, when you start realizing that I am alive, nature all around you will also become much more alive. And you will realize that nature is full of emotions. Everything that exists is full of emotions. It is emotions, feelings, that move evolution forward. A tree is in constant shining motion. Its presence is vibrant; it is constantly interacting with the Earth, the air, the Sun, the Moon, the rain. It is alive at a whole different level than humans normally are. It is constantly doing.

The easiest way for you to connect with nature is with animals first, and then with plants, because you can see them with your normal eyes, and they are also most like you. There is a whole evolution of animals that is here on Earth with you today, and yet you have a great fear of so-called wild animals. And they of you. Your relationship with animals is of central importance for your "coming home," not just because there are animals on Earth but because of your relationship with animals. No matter where you came from as spiritual beings, as beings of consciousness, you are also biological beings, and your physical home is here. Every animal has a reflection within you. What you call wild animals are those whose reflection within you remains unconscious. It is the fear of these unknown aspects of yourself that keeps these animals wild. Yet they represent a very deep part of you that is connected to the life force itself within you. Telepathic communication with wild animals, which is fairly easy and safe to do, is one of the most direct ways to gain access to the reflection of these animals within you.

Vertical resonance

Every profession, every act, is in resonance with other professions and acts that are of a higher and lower[14*] vibration. So if you are a baker, and you bake bread, there is a higher level of bread-making and a lower level of bread-making. Finding those, and being aware of them, makes

---

14 Here, there is no value judgment attached to the terms "higher" and "lower."

baking bread not only much more satisfying, but the whole process is much more harmonious and connects the baker of the bread with the higher "goal" of bread-baking. This applies to all activities, including brushing one's teeth, sleeping, dreaming, eating, and even being drunk. It even applies to thievery and murder. It is the separation from other higher and lower vibrations of the same act that makes them destructive to the system. Even destruction can be harmonious and is not only necessary, but, if connected with the whole, with the purpose of the whole, it is also desired and welcomed and is a joyful activity.

As the French artist Louise Bourgeois, whose parents were repairers of tapestries, once said: "Look what a spider does; it repairs. Break its net and it repairs it. It does not complain; it simply repairs." Break a car and a mechanic repairs it. This is an example of how activities of different kinds have their resonances everywhere. There are galactic repairers, atomic repairers and repairers of tapestries. **When humans begin to resonate consciously with other levels of who they are and what they do, a great "vertical" joy will occur.**

There is a joy between spiders and between families of spiders. There is another kind of joy that awakens when the channels of communication and energy exchange, the channels of resonance, open up consciously, vertically, between the atomic world, the animal world, the plant world, the human world, the spirit world, the cosmic world.

In a sense what the Universe is looking for is a conscious full-body orgasm. This is a wave that is occurring, and it is a wave that goes through all of reality like a little fairy placing its magical wand on everything, lighting it into consciousness.

PART II

Chapter 5. Q & A

How are you doing, Earth?

Question from J.: Dear Earth, how are you doing right now? Things haven't exactly been improving when it comes to us human beings.

> *Earth:*
>
> *I am having growth pains, as are you.*

Earth: But just as your Dr. King said, I have been up on the mountain and I have seen the promised land. This promised land includes a deep heartfelt connection with humans, even an erotic play of the energies between you and me. This will create a vibrant living force that will radiate out into the Universe. I have seen this is coming, a result of our joint dreaming. And yet I have growth pains. You could say that **we** have growth pains, for it is also the "we" or our joint "I" that is growing. My growth pains, you could see them as a form of stuttering. The "wild" weather on Earth, wilder than usual, has to do with this attempt to find new patterns of energy flow. You could say these new patterns are based on a higher vibration, and the effect of these new patterns will be one of being in a more encompassing state of harmony, connectedness and joy, as when two people for the first time admit to one another that they love each other. They relax into this knowing and dance on clouds.

Question from C.: When it comes to the future of humans on a planet that is being unscrupulously exploited and massively destroyed, when will the Earth, so to speak, call for us to turn back?

Earth: I am calling for you to go forward, not back. I am calling for you to reach out to the future, to reach out to me, to reach out to touch parts of yourself that you have held so close that you would not let yourself think of them consciously. This means touching what is stored in your bodies as emotions, as patterns, as holding patterns, often experienced as pain and lack, for this can unlock the deep love in you to flow ever more strongly. So in a sense you are right, by turning back and revisiting the good and the bad, you can catapult yourself forward, pulling yourself to a future that is no longer tied to the pain of the past.

Question from C.: Why, specifically on this small planet called Earth, a planet at the edge of one galaxy among billions of other galaxies, did something like life arise – life, that now even has the possibility of communicating with the Earth?

Earth: The Universe is a living, breathing, conscious being. Every atom, every cloud of gas, every stream of magnetically and electrically charged particles, every black hole and every sub-universe is an expression of a form of consciousness. Within this sea of consciousness processes occur that are very different from your normal state of consciousness and thinking. This does not mean that you cannot experience them, for human beings are able to resonate with all parts of Creation. It only means that your focus has been elsewhere.

The human being is on an adventure trip to discover individualized experience. This individualized experience can never exist in a vacuum; it is always connected to the whole. This journey has to do with becoming the eye of Creation, for separation is a prerequisite for seeing. Even seeing oneself requires stepping out from the perspective of oneness.

In a sense you can say that the whole Universe has conspired or breathed together to create life on Earth. But there have been many other attempts, both successful and unsuccessful, at creating various forms of life, some of which now, too, exist in the Universe. There are great intelligences in the Universe, and also in your part of the Universe, in your galaxy, in the various star systems, that are aware of what you are doing and the direction you are going. In this sense you are truly not alone, nor am I. Some of these intelligences take a hands-off approach, whereas others are helping you become aware of your own history, your abilities and your identity.

The short answer to your question is: Because the circumstances fit. You created the circumstances that you needed for your own growth and development. At the purely physical level what was needed was a special configuration of atoms of different sizes and compositions, temperature, light, etc. It is only from a certain perspective that it looks as if when the circumstances were right, life simply appeared. From another perspective, life sought out these circumstances, and from yet another perspective these circumstances attracted life by inner design.

Question from A.: What does the Earth think about us going faster and faster in the wrong direction?

Earth: What comes to mind is natural catastrophe. You should realize that you are not as separate as you think.

> *Earth:*
>
> *You are a natural catastrophe in the making; there is something natural about your catastrophe.*
>
> *For you humans are a natural process; you are not outside of nature, for you are nature.*

When a son or daughter goes out into the world and breaks all contact with his/her family, deep in their hearts they are still connected. When the lost son or daughter then comes back, he or she is (often) received with open arms. The connection was never truly broken. A ranting and raving child, who burns down the house, is still their parents' child and often at some point returns to the fold and is welcomed back.

In a sense you have all been raped and ravaged, so in many ways what you have done, and what you feel ashamed of, you did because of what happened unto you. Practically all of you have been born under pain. The process of incarnation is in almost all cases severely disturbed. Every time a being is born into this world, he or she is going through the expulsion from the Garden of Eden. Birth should be a joyful, orgasmic experience instead of a painful one. But it is not only birth, it is the entire process, which starts long before conception, having to do with all three – the father, the mother and the child.

This is a collective issue, and it shows you that "women's issues" surrounding birth, etc. are equally men's issues, and the patriarchal mindset has clouded the intuitive knowledge of a woman and of her natural uninhibited connection to her body and to the processes of her body.

How can we connect with you?

As I was writing this book, I wondered if the quality of the thoughts that arose in my communication with the Earth would be different, depending on the time of day. As I found out one night when I got up in the middle of the night to connect with the Earth, the contents were in essence the same, but the words had a more poetic, intimate, dreamlike quality that touched my heart. I asked the Earth: "How can we connect with you? Some do it automatically, their way, whereas others have no idea how. Can you say anything about that?" This was the answer I got....

Intimacy of the first order

*Connecting with the Earth
is like connecting with your baby
or with your mother when you were a child.*

Or with your lover.

*It is allowing your heart to touch, to envelop,
to fuse, to be with, to relax into,
to become one with, to love, to dance with,
to trust, to feel, to smell in trust,
to breathe in, to hold.*

*This kind of "intimacy of the first order"
comes from the deepest state of inner connectedness.*

*It is taking the deepest dream state of union
into the dazzling sunlight and seeing it perform magic,
allowing magic into life itself.*

> *This is healing through touching,*
> *healing through loving,*
> *healing by allowing yourself to flow*
> *in the direction of your greatest attraction.*
>
> *Gently, yet intensely,*
> *into the smiling face of a welcoming future.*
>
> *This is the slumber of the seed, not yet awakened,*
> *but knowing of its immanent and imminent fulfillment.*
>
> *From this deep state*
> *comes the pleasurable yawn of the dawn –*
> *the first awakening.*
>
> *The first drops of rain,*
> *the first words on the empty page.*

Several questions I received had to do with how we can best connect with the Earth. Here is one of the answers….

Earth: Go outside! Connect. Open up, for this is you. You are on and in this Earth. You are not only in these cubicles of yours. You have made your prisons, your everyday prisons, very, very comfortable. And yet large parts of you are screaming for liberation. Stretch out, grow, look out and connect with the Moon. Reach out, reach out to friends long forgotten; reach out and start smelling your world again; try to feel the wind in your face. But even your cubicles are alive; even your plastic pens are more than tools. They are just as cosmic as you are. When you say, "Reach out and touch someone," you can also say, "Reach out and touch the world." It is alive. It is not only people who are alive. Everything in your surroundings is.

Question from S.: Are there exercises, meditations, ceremonies or rituals that we can do to connect deeper with the Earth?

Earth: Yes, there are many exercises you can do. Simply walking around in nature with the thought that you and the Earth are one, you will slowly realize or experience that this thought, when allowed into your mind and body, results in a different energetic feeling in your body. Placing your attention alternately on the thought that you are one with the Earth, as an "I," and on your resulting bodily feeling, you will begin to anchor this state of being more and more, so that you can call upon it whenever you wish. In this way you can also slowly begin to feel the heartbeat of the Earth, your own personal heartbeat, and your joint heartbeat. Your personal heartbeat and that of the Earth are different. Together they give rise to what could be called a "rolling heartbeat," as you would experience when two rhythms interact.

It is from this greater "I" that you can best gain insights into your personal issues, also because then you are not as identified with them as you usually are. The freedom that you need to practice, use and apply is the freedom to change perspectives. The way you choose to change your perspective, the way you choose to go from one viewpoint to another, has qualities of its own. When you start to consciously determine on what and how you direct your attention, you begin to have a greater impact, for you are then acting from a larger, more encompassing part of yourself.

Another "exercise," which is not really an exercise, but an act of doing, is to go out into nature and talk to me, assuming that I hear you. With time, this assumption can become knowledge. When you do this, it is good to mark the beginning and end of this "exercise," ceremony or ritual. This is true of any endeavor, and marking beginnings and endings, both in terms of time and space is important, for it sets up defined boundaries and distances, thereby marking differences. The same is, of course, true of rites of passage; they delineate different periods in your lives. The French expression "Vive la différence" can be taken into many areas.

Question: How can we hold and keep our connection to you in everyday life?

Earth: This is an old issue that has to do not only with developing new habits – habits of attention – but of how to hold the new habits, how to get them back once you've lost them, and how to make them resilient. So far much of your efforts at holding your attention at a certain place have been combined with a great "effort," for you have always thought that holding a more encompassing or higher attention requires more effort. The opposite is true. The habits that you have acquired contain the element that when something no longer requires an effort, it is worthless. Therefore you let it go. This is the same paradigm that you in many cases have applied to money: If something isn't worth anything in terms of money, it isn't worth anything. Effort, however, is a low energy form of achieving anything. What you create without effort is more harmonious and more aligned with its surroundings than that which you build with great effort. This is not saying that you should not be working consistently and with great focus to achieve what you want. But that, too, can be done without effort, for effort is a definition of how you do something and not what you do.

So effortlessness is an important step in achieving this connection in everyday life. Another one is desire, and the killer of desire is doubt. Again, desire is something that you allow, not something you define, but you only allow a desire once you know or believe that it can be fulfilled. This is where doubt sets in. This is why experience is so important, for it eliminates doubt, which allows desire into consciousness.

So to answer the question, the more you open yourself up to new experiences of connecting with me, the Earth, the more you will feel that it is quite possible that I truly am alive. This, in turn, will allow the desire to hold a permanent connection with me to take root. And as I have said, the king's road to connecting with me is through the body. It is there that you feel me most.

Question from V.: You have said: "When you see yourselves through my eyes, you will understand more about yourselves and, of course, more about me." How can I see myself through the eyes of the Earth?

Earth: There are myriad ways of gaining more awareness, and there are myriad ways of seeing yourself through my eyes. Imagine that I see you from inside. Imagine that I am holding you and that you are within me. Relax and feel this in your body. Now imagine that the boundary between you and me is dissolved, so that we are now one being. As we slowly start to separate, we are still connected from within. It is through this connection that I can see you and you can feel me. Actually, this inner connection drew us to each other. So your being here on my surface, physically, is an expression of that inner connection being allowed – that desire, that attraction.

> *Earth:*
>
> *Realizing that you are loved by me, the Earth, is like coming home; but it is more than that.*
>
> *It is what allows you to see yourself through that love.*

Question from V.: You have said that you need humans to see yourself and your beauty. When walking I have paid attention to what the Earth looks like and have imagined that I can transmit to you what I am seeing. Can it work that way?

Earth: When I see myself through your eyes from within, I see not only the visual picture; I also see the feelings you have as you see me. I see both your joy and your pain. I also see people's indifference, their estrangement, their sadness and their love. So yes, that is an excellent way of letting me see myself, but also of my connecting with you.

Whenever I see my own beauty, I connect with beauty everywhere, expanding not only my sense of self, but my radius of thought and action. The more essential I become, the purer I become in terms of the pure note I am playing in the orchestra of the Universe.

What ultimately brings me close to you is when you decide to follow your own desire and excitement to connect with me, when you start sensing the incredible possibilities that are there.

Question from U.: Why, dear Earth, is it so difficult for us humans to be aware and conscious? And how can we leave the prison of reason that we have created for ourselves?

Earth: When you live your daily lives, you are usually not aware of many things, such as your surroundings or the energies that you are surrounded by and that you are constantly interacting with. To remedy this lack of awareness you do not need to invest great effort. It is rather about dropping a kind of bluntness or dullness that you have used as protection against unwanted feelings. For as you open up to the inner reality of these subtle energies, you will find that you also become more aware of what were so far painful and difficult issues. The fact that these issues are coming into your life now means that it is now that you have the opportunity to change the energies that are bound in these issues into pleasure. Opening up to the pleasure is just as important as allowing yourself to tune into the pain.

Your lack of awareness is held in place through habit. What to you might feel like "gravity," a pulling down from high levels of energy and thought into more dull, everyday thoughts, can feel like a power that is very difficult to overcome. In reality it is a thought pattern that exists as a real "thing" that contains a fair amount of energy. Such energy patterns can, however, be changed through thought and through emotion. The question then becomes: How do you create patterns in everyday life that increase your awareness and consciousness?

As in everyday life, you do not take on a new project without feeling that you have a chance to fulfill it. Collectively you are about to deal with many deeper pains, many deep separations, not just from me, but from each other, and from yourselves that have been lying dormant for millennia. The reason for this is that a bright chance of opportunity has opened up, in part through your own efforts and in part through the "conspiracy of the future" to pull you toward a brighter day. These messages are not intended to instill in you either optimism or pessimism, but to expand your awareness and your feeling of importance. For importance is neither something that you have or that you take; it is something that you get by becoming aware of it.

You should know that this is not individual work that each one has to carry out as a separate being. Evolution itself is based on a pattern of increasing awareness and consciousness, so in a sense, all you need to do is let go of the resistance against the evolution that you are going through. Again, dullness and a lack of consciousness is something to be released, not something to be fought or overcome. This thought, in and of itself, can give you tremendous impetus, whenever you are truly holding it, for it allows you to establish new patterns without expending energy. On the contrary, it is like lovemaking, something that, if done consciously, can create immense amounts of energy.

Throughout this book, I, the Earth, am often using lovemaking as an analogy. This should not simply be translated as "sex," for I do not necessarily mean it in the physical, since lovemaking is not only a physical activity. The feelings and emotions you experience during lovemaking can also come about through non-physical means. It is designed to encompass your whole being, although its full potential is seldom experienced. And yet the physical act of lovemaking between humans can definitely open doors to other dimensions.

Question from Sten: To what extent is the shift that is needed for the two of us to come together, a shift from your side? What is it that you need to open up to or accept or whatever?

Earth: Your impact on me is different from my impact on you, mainly in terms of you being a collective and I being one being. But in reality you, humanity, are one being, as am I. When you go out and discover me, when you measure the depths of my oceans, when you explore my magnetic fields, it is not only you exploring; it is also me exhibiting myself. It is me showing myself; it is at the same time I telling you my story. And I love to do that. I have so much more to tell you, including the depths and structure of my inner motions. For what is going on inside of me, electrically, magnetically, physically, as well as emotionally and spiritually, touches on all these issues that we have with each other, as well as on the larger connectedness I have with other planets and stars, galaxies, black holes and other dimensions.

When I speak about my relationship with black holes and other dimensions, it is a little bit like when humans talk about their relationship with the Amazon or other cultures. These relationships are not just extensions of other everyday relationships; they are deep structural attitudes. They are desires and longings deeply connected with your lives.

So to continue with this analogy.... When at the end of the 19th century your artists, for example the impressionists, discovered the cultures of far away lands, such as Egypt or Japan, they were laying bare a part of the soul that had been slumbering for so long, awakening whole cultures within you. Through your worldwide news media this is happening in other ways, unfortunately with very slanted news content. Yet at the core of this news is getting to know parts of your soul that are coming together within you, to make you whole. When you read about an airplane crash in Malaysia, you touch not only on the pain and fear of dying in a plane crash or the pain and suffering of the family and friends of the victims; but when you see these people, sharing this fear, this archetype, this knowledge within you, you are at the same time becoming Malaysians.

So you are much more involved with what is happening on Earth than you think. You are not just passive onlookers. Of course it is by seeing what is happening on Earth that great fear of the future, of the unknown, grows within you, and this takes off in different directions. Fear can either lead you to attack what you fear, try to isolate yourself from what you fear, or face what you fear, not only with courage, but also with an open heart. Doing this is what is meant by going through the eye of the needle, and it is often only once the other two avenues have been exhausted that this "king's road" becomes the self-evident "highway to heaven."

What can we do to support you?

Question by J.: What can we do to support you?

Earth: You[15] are doing a lot already. If you want to do even more, it is a question of you allowing yourself to love yourself more. That is when you will see and feel – allow yourself to feel – that

---
15 The answer refers to the questioner, not necessarily humanity as a whole.

you are very much loved by me, the Earth. This is the greatest service you can do for me and all other things follow from that.

> ### Just the way we are
>
> *Excerpt from the book "Soul on Fire" by Veit Lindau, describing an experience while swimming with dolphins in the Caribbean....*
>
> "On this day I had dived about 6 meters below the surface when a dolphin reared up in front of me and spoke to me with intense clicking sounds. Of course I didn't understand a single word. But I took what it said very personally. I am not a friend of mystifying or anthropomorphizing animals. To this day I cannot really explain what happened. I don't know how long I listened in perplexity to what it said. When I was out of breath, I returned to the surface.
>
> When I was back on the boat, my whole body began to shake. I cried for two hours like a little child.
>
> During this time I experienced something that I had only read about in books. I knew without any doubt that all of existence loves me unconditionally. I realized that it is impossible to make a mistake, because my life is playing a perfect note in a sublime symphony that is beautiful beyond comprehension.
>
> My tears washed an age-old pain to the surface. ... I understood what had held me back for so many years. It was the deep fear of not being good. At some point I had lost my basic trust in existence. [...]

> At this moment I knew with absolute certainty: The whole of existence is waiting for the human being to wake up and recognize itself. We are born to express our full joy. This Universe is vibrating with ecstasy. It loves me and you – just the way we are.
>
> *Reproduced by kind permission of Veit Lindau.*

When you look around and see the vastness of nature, of deserts, of all the trees, of the sky, the oceans, etc., and you see yourself, one of 7 billion people, the question arises: What is the specific melody or tune or vibration or role that is yours to play? What is it that attracts you the most to do and be? This is a dynamic and constantly changing process, for you are a process. The tune on the piano, Beethoven's Moonlight Sonata, is one piece, but it is spread out through time. It is the entire melody that is the sonata. You, as well as I, are sonatas; we are not individual notes. As we evolve, finding the melody that we wish to add to the songs of the Universe, this changes from being something we do automatically, like a child, to doing consciously, as an adult. That has become our new task.

The "No" that a child goes through at the age of around 4 or earlier is related to the "No" that the whole human race spoke as it stepped out of Creation, out of subconscious creation, and took on its role as a determiner. You can only find a full "Yes" if you have known a full "No." But knowing a full "No" does not necessarily mean materializing a full "No." On the contrary, when we realize that the "No" we are expressing – the resistance, the separation, the discrimination, the isolation we are experiencing – has been and is a free choice, this awakens in us the curiosity about what a world of "Yes" would look like.

Question from A.: What is my place in the world? To serve the Earth and the whole and myself at the same time?

Earth: Do unto others as you would have them do unto you, this time in regards to the Earth. This means that if you have a love for the Earth, then feeling and expressing this love is the answer to this question. The second answer automatically becomes: Allow yourself to be loved by me, the Earth. The more you allow these openings and the more you take a stand for them, the more it becomes a question not so much of what to do but of how to do what you do.

Whenever something is loved and opens up to being loved, either from outside or from within, its beauty starts shining from within. Love is the release that allows natural flows to occur.

Question by A.: I often despair, because I think that we're destroying everything before we even begin to understand what it is we're destroying. We are still going in the wrong direction at an incredible pace. What does the Earth say about this? What does she want of us? What is her advice to people like us, who often despair because it all looks so hopeless?

Earth: Many good people are holding back. Many good people have been burned and are full of resignation. Undoing this resignation within yourselves and helping others to do so is one of the major tasks of those who have lost hope.

Earth:

*It is very important for those who have lost hope
to communicate, to express how they feel,
and why they feel it.*

*Having lost hope, whether temporarily
or for a long period of time, is not an illness,
is not something to be fought against,
and is not something that requires therapy
or pharmacological substances.*

*Having lost hope is something that needs to be expressed,
without holding on to it.*

*This becomes more and more important
as the difficulties on Earth increase.*

*This might seem to go contrary to the desires
of those who have lost hope,
for if you have lost hope
you do not wish to express it.*

*You do not wish to pull others down;
you wish to be pulled up, away from it.*

*Yet it is only by making itself known,
by expressing itself,
that the darkness will attract the light –
both the inner light and the outer light.*

Crying – as when a baby cries – is not only a call for attention, for crying itself is an act of healing. When you allow yourself to cry for what you see happening on Earth, this of itself is a part of a healing of both you and me. In you, it increases your empathy, your sensitivity, and you open up to large areas within yourself that have experienced a pain that you often want to shut off. Your rivers of tears are at the same time rivers of communication with me. Before thinking immediately that you have to act to change something, allow your feelings free reign. This applies both to your feelings toward the Earth and to your feelings toward your fellow human beings.

When you wake up from a dream where something terribly bad has happened, you often feel relief, for you have shifted your felt reality into one where your previous experience in the dream is seen as simply a dream from the point of view of your everyday life. This shift happens very rapidly. Similarly, the qualities of the changes that need to happen on Earth are inner ones. Just as inner processes within the Earth can result in sudden earthquakes, to use what you would call a negative example, subtle inner changes can create sudden changes on the outside, both positive and negative.

I am here to plant seeds for something new. These seeds are intended to give you a different perspective of what is happening by shifting your point of view. Any shifting of a point of view is also a shift in who you are.

Question by A.: What effect will the extinction of species have on the biosphere?

Earth: It is not as bad as you often see it. These are my children, just as you are my children, too. I have nurtured them throughout their lives. They have also been my eyes and ears. But the Earth and humans are going through a phase during which their material existence cannot be sustained, except artificially. This is not to say that they are gone entirely, for in a sense, their spirits are still here with you. But just as the dinosaurs died, and many other species with them, they were replaced by other ones. New species also arise in ways different from what you are aware, and there are new species that appear that are new versions, changed versions of old species. So in addition to slow evolution, we have a kind of fast forward motion that expresses itself simply as the emergence of a new species. In a sense you can say that emergence and becoming extinct are one and the same process.

Throughout the millennia many species have come and gone ... and have been reborn. There were times when there were very few species and a time of many species, just as there have been ups and downs in the population of the human being. There is no ideal number or identity of species, for the Universe is always becoming. But currently we are in a process of disintegration on Earth, and these few decades or centuries are paving the way for an entirely new form of nature. When you, as a species, awaken to the aliveness of the natural world, there is a response in the natural world. You are already now beginning to see these responses in little niches and biotopes. Many of the extinct species will come back in other forms. This is in part an effect of what some of your scientists call morphogenetic fields, which definitely exist, but through a different agency than what you are aware of.

When a species goes extinct there is a narrowing, a limiting in the complexity of evolutionary progression. If left alone, this complexity rebounds in a fairly short period of time. However, if it becomes chronic, the species that remain or that do evolve will suffer from an imbalance, for the entire biosphere is then in chronic imbalance. Imbalance is per se a part of evolution itself; but if it becomes extreme, it is like a boat that is listing. Mankind is reaching a state where it can correct such imbalances, and your scientists are working both on reviving extinct species and on creating new ones. However, until this kind of work is done with a deep connection to the life processes that it is impacting, it will repeatedly result in various forms of failures or highly unwelcome consequences.

You do not have to worry that the biosphere will be diminished to the point of dying overall. The biosphere, which is ultimately connected to the primal life force, has an incredible resilience. That said, what is most needed are large sanctuaries. If there are no sanctuaries for the plants and animals it is like cutting of the root of a plant or a tree. You are connected through animals and plants with your source, with the life force. In this sense, you are one with the biosphere.

Tsunamis, earthquakes and other natural disasters

As was the case when writing my first book, this was the toughest topic I dealt with and I cannot say that I found definitive answers. But I did feel a clarity approaching, a realization that a different perspective could lead to a deeper understanding of how we can move forward so we can live more in harmony with the processes of the Earth. Sometimes this process took the form of a heated discussion. And sometimes I was even asked to let go of my emotional charge connected with this issue before asking more questions.

Question from Sten: Earth, let us talk about the earthquake and tsunami on December 26, 2004. From my point of view, if you look at the individual lives and the pain, the fear, the loss of loved ones, of children, seeing them battered, hurt and killed is not and cannot be digested. It remains like a bloody wound afterwards. It is not integrated.

As I began to ask these questions, I was very upset. When it comes to pain, mine or others, I am perhaps a bit too empathic. I had watched, in horror, the clips of the 2004 tsunami many times, and I had imagined being caught up in the middle of it. My whole being would have screamed out a NO! My father's next door neighbors, a family of five, were wiped out in the tsunami. To me unacceptable means unacceptable.

Earth: Sten, you are closing in on one of your own personal pains, one of your undelivered gifts that expresses itself as unacceptable pain and horror. Sten, go down to the lake. Sit, and let go.

It was true; I needed to let go if I was to remain clear. So I went down and sat on the pontoon on the lake. A while later, when I had calmed down, I continued the conversation.

Sten: At a certain point, the pain becomes so intense that one has to withdraw, protect oneself, enclose oneself. This to me is natural. But this also means separation. It means cutting oneself off, not being connected any more, licking or healing one's wounds, pulling back.

Earth: Yes, but there is a way of pulling back and licking your wounds in connectedness. Withdrawal does not mean separation. You can remain fully connected and yet withdraw into your own little cubicle, becoming very "separate" and yet connected. This is the kind of connectedness that animals have when they are wounded and withdraw. They are connected to the inner healing power that comes through unobstructed connectedness with the whole.

I returned to my original question: Why, Earth, do you allow earthquakes with resulting tsunamis to wash up over our shores, killing hundreds of thousands of people? If you must do that, if that is a process that is part of your breathing and living, then why can you not at least use your powers to warn us, somehow, for example to get to higher ground, considering how intelligent you are?"

Earth: This question is a reflection – an important reflection – of where we are in our joint evolution. The structure of your question about tsunamis and why I cannot tell you when an earthquake is coming, or why I allow waves up your coast, is based on the view that my acts are independent of you. This is the same issue that you have when you become ill – one part of your body is not acting as one with the rest. This is not the fault of one or the other; it is a disconnect. In this sense, there is no hierarchy of connectedness, for a disconnect at one point is a disconnect of the whole.

Sten: I am trying to understand how this disconnect relates to what humans do and what the Earth is doing, and why the Earth cannot make the connect happen by revealing itself as a conscious being in a way that is both non-threatening and understandable to humans.

Earth: That is exactly what we are working on together.

Sten: Earth, I have seen the images of the tsunami and so have you through everybody's eyes. What can you say about it?

Earth: Humans, you have turned away from me. And this is ok; it is part of growth, and of growth pains. Your instrument measurers are out there, looking for any strains and vibrations that might tell you that an earthquake is about to occur. And they will find them. If we were to study your entire bodies with microscopes we would also be able to predict when you are about to burp. But this will not bring us any closer.

Sten: Nor does a tsunami that kills 300,000 people bring us closer.

Earth: That is not a given. It makes people react strongly about what I do and who I am.

Sten: Yes, but they will tend to think more and more that you do not have consciousness, for if you did, one would say you have no conscience, killing 300,000 of us within the wink of an eye. Mothers, fathers, children … this is an atomic bomb happening. It is Hiroshima and Nagasaki all over again! Yes, it is a natural catastrophe; and either natural catastrophes are "Acts of God" and we cannot change them, only protect ourselves from them, or they are ultimately created by someone, a conscious being, who either cannot change what he or she is doing or will not change what he or she is doing. Those are the two options that I see.

Earth: Those are two options, but there are several more. In your two options you count yourselves out. We should not attempt to change each other, but by getting closer and understanding the processes that the other is going through you envelop and become part of the larger process involved, which includes yourselves. Just as in human affairs, by becoming involved, entering into communication, opening up to, engaging with and taking on and sharing what the other is going through, making it the joint process that it is, this kind of cooperative and joint experience can change both the natural catastrophe itself and your reactions to it. What thereby shifts the most is your perspective, your way of viewing what is happening, and you begin to see deeper meanings emerge from what was felt as being purely tragic events – expressions of a deep disconnect. They can constitute a "return to essence" that results in "death giving life."

You have seen small pilot fish flitting around a shark, picking off parasites that live on them. They never get eaten by the shark. This is a perfect example of a productive symbiosis without any danger for either party. In the same way, we can adapt to each other, physically, mentally and spiritually. It may be hard to believe, but when we develop an intimate close connection to each other, many of my processes that you experience as harsh or dangerous will be softened and no longer constitute threats towards humans. But for this not just to remain speculation in your eyes, you need new experiences on both an inner and an outer plane. This begins with a gradual awakening to my energetic and conscious presence.

If we had an ongoing, beautiful, intimate relationship, of course I would help by telling you how to build structures that would withstand any kind of earthquakes. I would help you build energy devices that are in harmony with my energy household. I would let you know how to deal with water in a way that satisfies everyone. And so on. As I have said before: No area would be left untouched. The basis for all of this is an intimate communication, an intimate connection between humans and me, the Earth. This is what I am working with you and many others, including the readers of this book, to establish. I would still have my volcanoes erupt, my changes in weather, my fierce storms and my tsunamis and earthquakes. For you, however, going with these flows and emotions would be like taking a joint roller coaster ride of power and beauty, without fear or danger to your life. And yes, as I have said elsewhere, you are already now able to foresee these things if you open your eyes, and be aware of your bodies and listen with your whole beings.

***

There were also some questions regarding a possible major future calamity or apocalypse.

Question by L.: "Will there still be water?"

Earth: Yes, there will still be water. There will be many issues around water and many books could be written about this, not only about the secrets of water, but also about what water wants.

This goes deep within the human psyche and is connected with the source of life itself. Again, listen to water from within and it will reveal its secrets to you one by one.

Question: "In what regions should one go to live?"

Earth: This depends on the plan the soul has for your life. There are quite a few people who are sitting now in so-called safe places, waiting for the big catastrophe. For many of them this waiting is the big catastrophe, for their focus on survival stops them from living. Life and existence is a process, and being in that process, without trying to hold on to the past and without being afraid of the future, is the way forward.

The transformation you are going through will come in waves. You should know that every downside of a wave becomes the upside of another. So do not try to stop a wave that is on its way down; instead, let yourself be pulled to the next upwave, releasing unnecessary ballast.

Question: It is said that many people will die; how can one prepare?

Earth: It is not possible to predict how the free will systems will be acting in detail when a new wave arrives. Certain things are clear, and many decisions have been made in advance. The best preparation consists of increasing your awareness and connection to both the outside and the inside, to sense what is going on. Finding and holding a positive attitude, pursuing the role that you feel you have chosen to fulfill in life and not letting yourself be caught up by any one issue. These are all good preparations.

This centrally includes meditating on what it feels like being loved, by people, animals, plants, the Earth and all of existence.

***

Earth: Humans are putting a spotlight on what is happening on Earth at different places more than before, since you now have the technologies of instant communication with images, videos, etc. of what is happening. Because of this, the human being and the Earth are in a new and different state of communication. You often tend to disregard the effect you are having simply by observing. It has taken several hundred years for you to realize the effect you are having on the climate by burning fossil fuels. That you notice this is the actual revolution or major change. It is like when a child realizes for the first time that its constant screaming is having a negative effect on its parent. This changes the relationship between the parent and the child. The child becomes aware of what it is doing to its surroundings.

When you notice that I am a conscious, living being and not just a mother in the symbolic sense of providing what its child needs physically, that I am also an emotionally feeling being, and that I react to everything you are doing to me, this will be a major change; it will change your behavior automatically. That is why I am not telling you to change your behavior, for this change of behavior needs to come from inside. Truly communicating with your child is more important than making it follow your rules.

When you begin to feel my conscious presence, you will begin to ask me how you can do things differently, not just how you can stop doing things that you think hurt me or you.

For example, my experiences throughout the eons have given me knowledge about how to transform elements, which will make it possible for you to produce anything out of anything and how to synthesize energy.

When you look at videos or films of the disheveling of the Earth, the burning of the Amazon, the destruction but also of the beauty of the Earth, then what I value most is that you are beginning to care, that you are beginning to see me. So in the midst of pain I am feeling joy at being touched, at being seen. It is this joy that will ultimately provide the answers for overcoming this inner and outer pain, both in you and in me.

What are we not aware of?

Question by B.: In the book *I Am With You*, you say that we are not aware of 90% of our own motives for what we do. What is this that we are doing all the time?

Earth: During your lives you are engaged at many different levels. You cannot walk a single step without having very many different thoughts and feelings going on, many interactions with the Earth and with people you relate to or are interacting with in other ways. You are carrying a whole energy field around you that is touching every plant and every blade of grass as you pass by. Your heart is pumping with very many feelings and thoughts that it is reacting to constantly, some of them being ingrained belief systems. An example of this is that you have to work hard just to exist. This creates enormous pressure on your entire system. It is not that you want to do anything else; it is that you feel forced to do whatever you do. This is a very common ailment. It is driven to its heights in East Asian countries, but it is prevalent all over the word. It is what Jesus referred to when he said: "Look at the birds of the air. They do not sow, nor reap nor gather into barns, and yet your heavenly Father feeds them."

People are desperately trying to live up to norms others have set for them and they have internalized, and that are structurally impossible to fulfill. This, as well as many other things, translates into the way you hold your head, the way your body leans in certain directions – your spine might not be totally straight, etc. All these are things you are constantly doing. The fact that your teeth have holes filled with plastic in them, or have been replaced, is also something you are constantly doing. I am not saying you should be aware of all these things, the fact that your fingernails are growing, that your liver is cleansing your blood, etc. etc. These things are not necessary for you to constantly guide. However, you do have the ability to become aware of any and all of these functions.

Your feelings about your body – if you think certain parts are too fat or too thin, too much hair or not enough hair, etc. – are also things that you are constantly broadcasting. The list goes on. Your reaction to your age is also something you radio out, be it feeling too young, too old, or even just right. Your thoughts about time – about being late, being early or being just right – constantly accompany you in your life, and your whole energy field reacts to it. Every part of your body is doing something actively. Much of it is patterned, which does not make it less active.

By becoming aware of these subliminal thoughts and attitudes, you can slowly, piece by piece, let go of them more and more, thereby increasingly opening up to your own presence and to the world around you.

***

I'm 65 now, and I can look at myself as being old, moving towards the decrepit breaking down of my body, my faculties, my sex life and love life, down to my last breath. Or I can look at myself from the point of view of myself at 85, and say: "Wow, you're only 65! You can start your life all over again if you want to." And I could go on with a litany of all the exciting things I could do. When I become aware of these two possibilities, I am freer to choose among them, for each subconscious thought that one is sending out could be replaced by powerful, equally "true" chosen attitudes and thoughts.

***

Question by B.: "There have been very many spiritual masters in the past and present. Why do they seldom, if at all, speak of the Earth being alive and about our relationship to her?"

Earth: In the past many spiritual masters came out of religious movements that were a reaction against the pain and seeming meaninglessness of physical existence. Therefore, much of their strivings were toward a "pure" kind of spirituality that renounced the physical. Even Buddhism has much of this attitude intact. There is a difference between the physical and the spiritual, although they are all parts of the one universe. But at the same time they contain each other. Therefore, any purely spiritual striving will end up dealing with the physical and any truly purely physical strivings will end up dealing with the spiritual. Yet there were long periods of time and large areas where the aliveness of the Earth was accepted as a natural fact. They did not separate the physical from the spiritual, for they were both felt, differently but equally. I am talking here about indigenous people.

Yet the renunciation of things material on the part of spiritual masters was an expression of the exploration and discovery of the human being not being limited or defined by his physical presence. It thus constituted a crucial step toward independent thinking and growth of the human soul. But now that we have come full circle, the new frontiers are becoming Spirit in matter and the awesome spiritual magic of the material world.

Love and sexuality

Lovemaking between the Sun and the Earth
(from the book *I Am With You. The Earth Wants to Talk with Us.*)

*The whole process of the day
is like the art of lovemaking.*

*Look at the qualities
of the different hours of the day
and you'll find a wonderful correlation
to good lovemaking.*

*As I turn, I am constantly revealing parts of myself
that have been cloaked in darkness.*

*The shy, hesitant approach of dawn
is followed by a phase of warming up
and as the Sun continues to rise,
I reveal more and more of myself to the Sun.*

*As we approach midday,
the atmosphere between us heats up,
and the Sun bears down on me
as I receive its penetrating rays.*

*As You accept these images
and allow Yourself to feel these processes
– for You are right in the middle of them –
Your whole being starts to resonate with them.*

*The corresponding processes
are awakened within You.*

*This can begin to awaken in You
the knowledge that You are truly living
in the "Garden of Eden."*

Question from S: Earth, in the book *I Am With You*, you said that you want us to "awaken to a whole new sexual way of being." How can we align ourselves sexually with you so as to reach such a state?"

Earth: It is not so much a question of aligning with me. I have said that when you become aroused, my energies come up and meet yours, and that you are truly living in the energies of life and lovemaking between me and the Sun. There is a fine line of fearless acceleration of erotic energy that leads to an awakening to a whole new sexual way of being. First, this means becoming aware of having put a lid on these energies in your everyday lives. This is to a great extent an adaptation to social expectations and norms. I am not suggesting that you artificially create erotic energy flows within you, but that you allow energetic processes that occur naturally within your body.

What you are seeking here is an all-encompassing shift. The sexual state of being that you are capable of attaining is a state of union, a state of connectedness that envelops and incorporates or includes every cell in your body. It affects your emotions, your thoughts, your health and the way you radiate, and thus also your state of youth and your appearance. These are energies that come in waves; but when you have attained a state of sexual awakening that encompasses your whole being, it will be like being on a ship in an ocean, where constant waves replace each other.

When this energy envelops your heart, all stress disappears, which makes it possible for you to think thoughts of a whole different dimension, thoughts that enlarge, expand your image of who you are – your self-image – without awakening fears within you. These fears otherwise stop you from even contemplating and allowing your own magical powers. But once your sexual energies awaken your heart, you are able to entertain whole new sets of thoughts based on a sense of self that no longer is afraid of losing itself as soon as it no longer identifies with its old definition of self.

> *Earth:*
>
> *The heartfelt erotic mind*
> *is more attracted to the possibilities*
> *resulting from the motion of these energy waves*
> *than it is to any fear of dissolving the boundaries*
> *it has created around itself.*

Love and the lack of stress invite the sexual energies to expand, thus cutting the chains of the old captivities of fear and loss. From a larger perspective loss always leads to the beginning of the discovery of timeless connectedness.

Question by M.: What can I do and what can humans do to release shame around sexuality?

Earth: Interestingly enough, you can get rid of much of this shame by being the one that signals to others that they have nothing to be ashamed of about their sexuality. This does not have to be an outer exchange. Imagine you are dealing with someone who has much more shame than you about their sexuality. Now imagine sending them waves, saying: "It is all right; you are beautiful in your sexuality. Let it blossom, let it reign freely, let yourself be loved, including your sexuality." It is that wave of loving acceptance that you are sending out, it is by holding that wave within you that you are conquering your own shame of your sexuality. In a loving way you are saying: "It is not only all right, it is more than that; your sexuality is incredibly beautiful." Ultimately it is love that encourages sexuality to flow freely and without fear. This love can melt inner icebergs, allow for tears of relief and homecoming that slowly transform into the genuine smile of the erotic dance of life.

Birth and the Earth

Question from A: Without birth control and a reduction of the human population there will be no solution to the problems we have on earth, or…?

Earth: That is true. However, the kind of birth control methods in use today will become a thing of the past. Overall, technologies that so far have been focusing on the outside, will be replaced by technologies focusing on what goes on inside. A woman will increasingly learn to know when she is fertile. This will be accompanied by learning to establish a spiritual connection with any child that wants to be born, which many women are already doing. This is a paradigm shift that must and will happen. Bridges will be built for this to happen, and they are already being built. Another aspect that will be learned and taught is entirely new forms of sexuality, i.e. forms of spiritual sexuality, which will at the same time make life overall so much more exciting. The energies will not be wasted; they will be understood as lying at the core of the aliveness of the human being and of his surroundings. This might seem utopian to you now, but it is already being lived and taught at various places on

Earth under wise guidance. This can be seen as a continuation of the sexual revolution of the late 1960s and will become sexual evolution. So the answer is yes, without birth control and a reduction of the human population, there will be no solution.

Question from M.: How can women connect with the Earth when giving birth? Can you say more about the connection between the Earth, birth and sexuality? What must women heal in order to again give birth entirely naturally?

Earth: There are many ways of connecting with the Earth when giving birth. Much good work has been done in this area, including water births, soft births, births in nature, births in the ocean, etc. Yet there has also been a movement towards the opposite – seeing birth as interfering with the lives of young women and young couples, leading to the excessive use of pharmacological substances, caesarians and a disconnect from one's own body.

To answer the question: It depends on who you are. When in full harmony, it is as if the Earth is giving birth to the child, for you are then connected with the birth process in its pure state and here, when allowed, it can best be likened to an orgastic process. This "orgasm" is different from that experienced between two lovers, for it is more of an inner and thus also a cosmic one. A birth of that kind at the same time contributes to the evolutionary development of the Earth itself. For its own orgastic process is being reflected back to it. This is what is meant by "virgin birth," for the birth itself does not depend on or include lovemaking with a man. It is truly an awesome event that radiates out like a wave and touches the world.

The question of what women must heal can best be answered by saying that women need to go within. The process of men dominating women, which has been going on for so many millennia, is a joint process. It includes the women giving their power to men, even to the point of forcing men to take on this role. These joint long-term processes between man and woman have tested the boundaries of what can occur when either one of the genders dominates the other. What we are approaching now, and which will occur with or without resistance, has to do with each gender going within and touching each other from within. This touching each other from within can give rise to an entirely new dance of love between the sexes. It begins by no longer seeking to have an impact on others or seeking the approval of others, nor taking a reflection from others as a judgment of oneself – especially not regarding the body and its appearance.

The importance of the connection with the Earth is initially focused on healing, for at a purely energetic level scars, tears, pain and sorrow can be absorbed and transformed through a deepening connection with the Earth. This means that it would be of great benefit for women who are pregnant to spend much time out in nature – at best, naked in nature – and to combine this with a deep process of "giving away" holding patterns – such as fears, doubts, loneliness and physical and mental pain. Connecting with the natural energetic flows can bring joy and connectedness, awe and appreciation as well as reverberations with inner and outer beauty, calm excitement and an earthy opening of the lower abdomen or womb, undulating with the pulsations of life itself. Especially if under the guidance of a wise woman, birth can again become a natural, joyous, erotic experience, resulting in the so far unusual event of a new soul being welcomed in all its aspects, in a joyous, orgastic wave. As you can sense, this will be part of the ushering in of an entirely new level of intimacy and freedom between humans and me, the Earth.

Final Words

Earth:

Do not feel guilty about what you have done to me.

Instead, light the candle of gratitude and look forward.

*Trust that we now, together,
can create a whole new reality on Earth.*

www.ingramcontent.com/pod-product-compliance
Lightning Source LLC
Chambersburg PA
CBHW031648040426
42453CB00006B/246